A YEAR IN SILVERDALE

*Observations of natural life in and
around this Lancashire village*

~

Richard Norman

Illustrated by Sue Thompson

'Oh for a lodge in some vast wilderness'
William Cowper – *The Task*

HELM
PRESS

For Celia

Published by Helm Press
10 Abbey Gardens, Natland, Kendal, Cumbria LA9 7SP

Tel: 015395 61321

E.Mail: HelmPress@natland.freeserve.co.uk

Copyright – Richard Norman and Anne Bonney

First Published 2004

ISBN 0 9540497 8 0

Typeset and printed by
MTP Media Ltd, The Sidings, Beezon Fields, Kendal. Cumbria LA9 6BL

Front cover: Waterslack Lane

Contents

Foreword

A fascinating insight into one man's daily observations of wildlife and the changing seasons throughout the year. The fact that Richard has chosen the area around his home as the focus of attention ensures we are treated to an incredible variety of wildlife, as this corner of North Lancashire and South Cumbria is incredibly diverse and he obviously rejoices in this fact. This is well illustrated by Richard as he effortlessly takes us from the daily happenings in his garden, involving the types of wildlife familiar to millions, through to such specialised wildlife haunts as Leighton Moss and Morecambe Bay, with such exotic wildlife as marsh harriers, bitterns and thousands of oystercatchers.

Richard's style enables the reader to feel as though they are at his shoulder sharing in all his observations. The descriptions of the vagaries of the British weather and how they affect ones emotions will strike a chord with everyone; such as the way a sunny morning can lift the spirits even in the depths of winter.

The text is liberally sprinkled with country folklore and insights into the lifecycles of all manner of wildlife. By the end, one is left feeling as though one has had a personalised guide to the comings and goings of the wildlife in and around Richard's home.

If you want to know why so many people venture out into the countryside, often in inclement weather then read this book and the passion it awakes deep within us is plain to see.

Robin Horner
Senior Warden
R.S.P.B. Leighton Moss and Morecambe Bay Nature Reserve

July 2004

Introduction

I developed a keen interest in natural history as a young boy roaming the fields and woods of my native Staffordshire. After leaving school at sixteen I worked in various jobs before going to read English at Lancaster University as a mature student. I subsequently settled in the area and lectured in English at Preston College. On taking early retirement from teaching I devoted myself full-time to bookselling in the shop I owned with my wife. I am now retired and have had time to write this book on Silverdale, the area in which I live and love.

The illustrator, Sue Thompson, lives in Kendal and has been a Lake District National Park Ranger for fifteen years and has an obvious love of nature.

The village of Silverdale stands in well-wooded limestone country on the shores of Morecambe Bay. In former times its people made a living from farming and fishing, from the export of local mineral products and from the movement of cattle by ship from Galloway, in southwest Scotland, down into England. There was also a steady traffic of people crossing the sands at low tide on foot, on horseback or in horse-drawn vehicles to the Furness region of Lancashire and to the Lake District beyond.

These activities are largely vanished now, though they have left their mark on the landscape and in local place-names, lore and legend. The land itself has survived the centuries unspoiled, having been protected by its surrounding hills, its tracts of marshland and the powerful tides and treacherous sands of the Bay.

Within the confines of a relatively small area there is a great diversity of geographical features and wildlife habitats. There are tide-washed sea marshes, extensive mud flats at low tide, sheep pasture, flower meadows, limestone pavement, scrubland, tall cliffs in disused quarries, one very deep lake, the extensive reedbeds of Leighton Moss full of rare and attractive bird life, and, most notably perhaps, a wealth of deciduous woodland. The countryside hereabout is of such a special quality that it is designated an Area of Outstanding Natural Beauty, with its own body the Arnside and Silverdale A.O.N.B. Trust, as its guardian. Important national bodies, The National Trust, English Nature and The Royal Society for the Protection of Birds, are all landowners here, custodians of the remarkable richness of landscape and the huge variety of wild things living in it.

We are all, in our different ways, responsible for the safekeeping of our natural heritage. This book, an affectionate portrait of the Silverdale landscape and its wildlife, is part of my contribution. It is a personal view, a record of the changing seasons and a celebration of the natural world.

Richard Norman

Richard Norman

Red Bridge Wood in Winter

January

New Year's Day

Janus, the two-faced god of the ancient Romans after whom the month is named, looks upon much the same weather at the beginning of the month as he can see in the concluding days of last year. Several days of hard frost, compounded with a dusting of snow, provided us with a crisp, white morning. We celebrated the end of the old year with fireworks just in front of the house in last night's bitter cold, hurrying indoors for hot food straight afterwards. This morning the spent cases lie scattered on the frost-bonded gravel, waiting to be gathered up.

After breakfast I sat with my two grandchildren just before they left with their parents for the long journey south. They had been given fancy party hats made of card last night, the last of the season, and after some discussion decided that the boy, five, was going to be a guard and look after his sister, seven, who would be the princess. Her royal highness was content to sit in quiet and undisputed majesty and demand regally to be fed with a fictitious but indisputably grand banquet of sausage, chips and beans. I gave them my loyal undertaking that whilst they were far away in their castle by the sea on the south coast, I would look after their northern fortress for them, their lodge in the enchanted forest, which is in plain and unadorned truth our house standing at the edge of its acre and a half of wood.

They were away before ten, and the day remained quite a reasonable one, giving the travellers time to complete much of their journey before dark. But here in Silverdale a freezing fog descended at half-past two, hiding the enchanted wood and the solitary guardian who walked in it. I hastened indoors to sit reading by a good log fire. No point having your own wood if you don't make use of some of it now and then. The poet John Clare puts the idea very well in his incomparable poem of the country year, 'The Shepherd's Calendar':

> *Withering and keen the winter comes*
> *While comfort flies to close shut rooms.*

2 January

Our Anglo-Saxon ancestors called January the Wolf Month because the wolves came closest to man's habitation and his flocks in this coldest of months. The last wolf in England, according to legend, was slain not many miles away, just across the Bay on Humphrey Head. Until then the threat of meeting one in the heaths and woods was real, not just a thrilling element of a child's tale. Even now the hardness of the earth and the chill winds blowing through the village bring to mind the bleakness of the winter landscape in the middle ages and the harshness of existence for people long ago, when they had more than just cold weather to contend with. The month itself seems wolfish in its character even today.

3 January

Bitter cold again, everyone longing for the time when the hard and rime-encrusted hazel catkins or 'lambs' tails' will be three times the length they are now, loose and dancing in a less bitter breeze. Even against my south-facing wall the gnarled old damson trees show no signs of life, yet are beautiful in their spareness and contortion of form. Their scaley and lichen-encrusted bark and twisted branches would be my entry for the Turner Prize, though it would never win, being altogether too real, too positive, too beautiful. In any case 'found' objects are presumably not permitted, only distortion that has been laboured at.

4 January

The cold continues. Roe deer come into my wood for shelter and for food, up to five at a time. We are in the territory of one particular roebuck, who is normally accompanied by two does and one half-grown kid from last season, born in our wood. They are watchful always, but not particularly fearful when they detect our presence, and this severe weather naturally makes them bolder in their foraging. The wild birds also take little heed of us as we stand close to the kitchen window watching their antics on the nut dispensers just the other side of the glass or on the bird tables only a few feet away. Later a kestrel sat on a telephone wire leading to the house. She knows there are mice and voles about and not all in hibernation, but it is going to be hard for the mouse hawk to find her dinner in the present weather

Twelfth Night

A thaw set in yesterday, but the accumulated layers of a week's frost took some time for the steady rain to wash away, so hard was the ground underneath. By this morning it had all gone; the turf was soft again and the wood and the garden, instead of being bound in iron by the frost were wrapped softly in a cloak of thick mist, through which our resident cock pheasant gave a querulous call, an incongruous sound like the working of a mechanical toy. He is a very distinctive bird, with a broad white collar and a wine-red rump, very confident and unafraid, coming regularly to the door to be fed with grain. He is coming up to his fourth season with us, having survived passing traffic, autumn shoots, hungry foxes and all manner of other hazards. As he is nearly one of the family, we have given him the noble and distinguished name of Cedric. He responds by making our wood the heart of his territory, like the deer.

The wood is only an acre and a half in extent, but the trees continue beyond our property and on to the golf course. Indeed our little wood is, from an animal's point of view, more or less continuous with Eaves Wood and part of the great tract of woodland that extends, with a few breaks, from Arnside Knott to Warton Crag, from Beetham down to Jenny Brown's Point. Much of this woodland stands on limestone pavement, a vast extent of which surrounds the broad tidal waters of Morecambe Bay. Our own limestone was partially plundered in the past, but a preservation order rescued it, and nature quickly covered the blemishes. A sort of ridge or hog's back of limestone runs right up the middle of our wood, bristling with the thickest growth of trees. Here the roe deer rest sometimes, though less so in the winter. I didn't notice them this morning until I had drawn level with where they lay completely still and unconcerned. My two dogs, Toby (bull terrier) and Blossom (Pyrenean Mountain dog), helped neither by scent nor movement, remained completely unaware of the deer that we left undisturbed as we passed on.

7 January

Woodcutting going on all day in my wood, a team of three thinning out the trees, mainly sycamores with one spindly oak and an ash or two in those areas where the densely packed mass needed thinning to give the remaining majority room to grow. This small-scale clearance is also important because it will let more sun and air in to help the spread of the woodland flowers such as primroses and bluebells.

In days gone by the wood's silence would have been broken by the steady thump of the woodsman's axe, but now the characteristic sound of woodcutting is the self-justifying whine of the chainsaw. 'The shortness of man's days will not allow him to cut down many trees' wrote that great Victorian naturalist, Richard Jefferies, but now one man can cut down an entire forest in his lifetime, with results which would have appalled Jefferies, as they appall us. Times change, further proof of which is that the three woodcutters were all girls, or I suppose I'd better say young women, but that is one innovation which can only be applauded. And in a most professional manner did Liz, Sue and Rebecca go about their work, stacking the newly-felled lengths of timber under standing trees to season, whilst seasoned lengths from previous years were chopped into logs for winter fires. Here again there was novelty, and even the all-powerful chainsaw had been superseded, by a Swedish log-chopper, a new machine with a conveyor belt and powerful jaws to cut the timber into chunks of just the right size for my fireplace. The pile of logs grew into a young mountain, with heaps of sawdust as the foothills. The twigs and thinner branches, the 'brash' as they are called, were taken to one side for burning at a later date, though a start was made this afternoon with some of it, a thin column of smoke the colour of a ringdove's feathers ascending into the thickening fog of early evening.

12 January
Thick mist along the valley this morning, so that stands of trees looked like remnants of a drowned forest. The rising sun, wrapped in mist, peered like a reddened eye over the shoulder of Warton Crag. It shone thinly among the trees in my wood, becoming a magic shield caught by some enchantment and hung up in the lost forest to await its wandering owner's return. This fairy-tale mood evaporated later when the sun succeeded in burning off the mist. The day became a sunny one. I watched the birds down at Barrow Scout Fields, the level fields between Crag Foot and the sea-marshes, mostly greylag geese that are commoner than they used to be and gather hereabouts for the winter as well as breeding at Leighton Moss. It is one of those grand spectacles of nature in these islands, a skein of wild geese dark against a grey wintry sky or coming in to land on the fields and marshes in the pale winter sun. Not for the first time I wished I could draw. The late Sir Peter Scott wrote that the reason he enrolled at the Royal Academy was to learn to paint wild geese better, to show something of their freedom, their beauty of form and grace of movement, the magnificent wildness of the places they inhabit.

A big flock of lapwings also descended on the marshes. They are numerous here in winter, and breed in local pasture where the grazing isn't too intensive and the grass cutting isn't too early. The plight of lapwings is not as bad as it is elsewhere, numbers having declined nationally in recent years. Even in these parts there are grave hazards, however. The building of one local supermarket, some years ago, robbed a couple of dozen pairs of these birds nest sites. Building, pollution, agriculture: there are so many ways in which the wild things are affected by the pressures of the human population expanding beyond the capacity of the land to support it.

20 January

A lone curlew flung across the grey sky by the strong wind, giving that plaintive, lilting wail which speaks straight to the human soul of barren moors, windswept saltmarsh and frost-locked fields. Perhaps the call was a cry for companionship, a beacon like most bird noises. Curlews often fly in groups: where in the vast emptiness of the sky were his fellows?

A solitary crow was also being buffeted by the wind, but his more robust and defiant calls resulted in a reunion with his group of half a dozen. Perhaps they were a family party, the result, even, of crows breeding in our wood these last three or four years. Each season a pair, probably the same pair, returns to the wood and builds a nest in the same part, on the eastern edge looking out across the sheep fields towards Hawes Water and the disused quarry at Trowbarrow. Off the party went, tumbling through the air and cursing amiably at what even they couldn't quite control.

Crows are about the only birds I know which seem to relish bad weather. I remember years ago one very hard frost in the mid-sixties lasting for weeks and killing large numbers of birds of all sorts. Those that still lived kept under cover, creeping out to seek a few scraps of food during the few hours of half-light that passed for day-time. The carrion crows, presumably, did not go short and for once could live up to their name, but even a full belly and the absence of hunger hardly explain why I was able to watch half a dozen of them out skating on the surface of a big reservoir over which the ice had formed several inches thick. While all the other birds were huddled in bushes, chilled and moribund, and life in general was at a-low ebb, these crows were slipping, sliding and cackling in apparent delight out on the ice, a hundred yards from any cover and with no prey or food of any sort within sight. Their sole purpose for being where they were appeared to be amusement.

21 January

Crows again. Fifty of them in the fields near the level crossing, a big winter congregation surprising to anyone used to the idea of them being a solitary species. Rooks, we know, are used to communal living and are dejected when excluded from it. Jackdaws breed together and spend much of their time in the winter in large groups, feeding. Only the other day another group of fifty, out in a foraging party from Trowbarrow Quarry, perched in the big oak against my front wall, eyeing the seed I had scattered on the ground for all comers. Even magpies sometimes go about in large groups at this time of year, but crows? They go about in couples only, surely, or twos and threes at most. But like most other crow species they have their gatherings, and today this big flock searched the turf diligently for worms, leatherjackets and other delicacies, proving their usefulness to agriculture. I can't help feeling their sinister reputation is largely unjustified.

There must certainly have been more than enough worms about for the crows today and when I went out with my dogs this evening it was mild enough for considerable earthworm activity on the lawns. I went into the wood towards midnight and found scores of them lying out on the grass, having their own get-together. It's perfectly normal to see this activity in the spring and summer, but it does seem strange in January. After all, it is only a few days since they were shut into the earth by the frost. All the more reason for them to be out and about now, I suppose, some completely out of the earth and others firmly anchored in their burrows, ready to whisk out of sight at the vibration of my footfall or the beam of my torch falling on them. They were all busily engaged in feeding on the wet leaves which plastered the surface of the damp ground, leaves which earlier in the day, before the rain came on, were being bowled along by the wind.

There is something fascinating about this secret, silent mass-dining-out in the pitch dark by creatures normally never seen except after rain or when digging the garden, when like as not we accidentally sever a worm with our spade and the two, poor, sundered halves wriggle apart, at least one of them to grow again its missing segment, we hope, though the robin in a bush nearby will have other ideas.

22 *January*

The milder weather continues, and I went to see if I could find any snowdrops in my garden, where they had appeared by the third week in the month last year. Somehow I feel the year has properly begun when the first snowdrops are out, but all I could find was their leaves bristling like a mustering of green spears and two or three white heads warily peering out of their sheaths. I know some people already have some of their snowdrops out, and the first lambs have been seen tottering in the fields, but though it is quite natural to yearn for these familiar and re-assuring sights of a relenting season, I am quite content to wait my turn and let events unfold around me, to let the wild things cross my path rather than always to seek them out.

When I lived in Warton I was able to grow yellow aconites under a hawthorn hedge, in the merest strip of soil which scarcely merited the name of front garden, and they were the earliest sign of new growth and the most welcome sight of the late winter, a bursting forth of gold from the cold, dark earth, like stored sunlight. Curiously, they won't grow in my garden here in Silverdale, where nothing poetical presents itself at the minute, only the homely growths of the first rhubarb, a couple of ruby sticks with unfolding, corrugated leaves of a lettuce-green.

Under another protecting wall, beneath the overhanging sloe bushes, a vigorous but unobtrusive plant with strange smelling leaves shaped like the feet of moorhens. This plant bears the unenviable name of the stinking hellebore, and it is a plant of some robustness of character, which it needs to have to carry off such an uncomplimentary appellation and not die of shame. It flowers from now until the end of April, and will see out the snowdrops and most of the daffodils. Its flowers are already showing green and cup-shaped with maroon edges like lipstick smears on a teacup. Its seeds are curious three-horned capsules, and begin to ripen in about three months from now. The seeds are spread in the usual way, by the splitting of the capsule, but snails help in the spread of the plant by eating an oily substance secreted on each seed, leaving the seed itself alone but sticking to its slime, by which means it is carried along. This explains why a new plant suddenly springs up six or eight feet away from the parents.

23 January

A green woodpecker flew into the garden, probably from Eaves Wood, where ants – its favourite food – are in very short supply. It dug vigorously with its sharp beak in the thick grass around an old tree-stump close to the house, where we watched it from our landing window. When its distinctive red head was out of sight in the grass the bird was very well camouflaged in its cloak of green. It was feeding on insect grubs and wintering adults. A great spotted woodpecker regularly visits our bird tables, where it is a welcome and colourful, almost exotic, sight, but the green woodpecker normally only comes to us in the summer, when there are plenty of ants for it to feed on.

27 January

Gales in the night. The rain had stopped by dawn but the high winds carried on, keeping some birds grounded. In the big field opposite a party of four mistle thrushes fed on the variety of insects and their larvae that attracts various species almost on a daily basis. My attention was distracted by something else, and after looking away for just a few seconds I found the thrushes had turned as if by magic to a party of seven magpies, hopping and flirting and seeming to care little of the wind that blew their long tails sideways. This is the time of year when the 'magpie marriages' take place, with up to forty or fifty of them, sometimes more, gathering together for, so naturalists believe, the purposes of courtship. This seems likely, as with up to half the magpie population remaining unmated in any year, partly because of the availability of suitable nest sites, a forum or meeting place helps single birds to find a mate and paired birds to confirm their relationship.

The wind continued, and significantly the kestrels were hunting from trees and telegraph poles today, not hovering. I watched a little male on a half-grown ash along Ford Lane, and later a larger female, all brown and lacking the grey head and tail of the male bird, as she also perched on a fence post rather than flew, on the watch for the slightest movement in the grass betraying the presence of a mouse or vole.

The water birds seemed less concerned by the wind. I watched them down at Crag Foot, where a year or so ago several fields were bought by the Royal Society for the Protection of Birds, whose ambitious and entirely creditable plan it is to return the grazing to its original state of marsh and reedbed, a sort of extension of Leighton Moss nearby. For centuries Man has been draining marshes and water meadows, to the point where wetlands have become scarce enough to restrict and depress the populations of some of our most fascinating and beautiful species of birds, not to mention rare plants and insects. This project is of the utmost importance nationally as well as locally, and is an island of good news in a slimy sea of environmental destruction. Shallow channels were cut into the soft and watery ground last year, as the first stage of what is a long process of restoration involving the planting of reeds, the management of water levels and so on. Already the birds have taken advantage of the wetter conditions, with today a mixture of wigeon, teal, mallard and shelduck swimming on the temporary lake that has obliterated the channels, and redshank, oystercatcher and curlew probing their long beaks into the muddy margins.

28 January
There are few compensations in being the sort of light sleeper who sometimes has a wakeful night. One is being able to read without interruptions from visitors or the telephone; another is seeing the dawn breaking in all its crystal purity, or being able to watch nature at work even in the middle of the night. At two o'clock this morning I saw the unmistakeable shapes of two roe deer grazing under the twin oaks on our front lawn by the light of the full moon, which was shining briefly through a gap in an otherwise thick covering of cloud. They, too, were wakeful, but deer can please themselves what hours they keep, without reference to custom and the convenience of others. They can stay awake for long periods at night, and like to rest during the day when they can, often doing so in our wood where they know they are not likely to be disturbed. I have seen them, in a group of three or four, lie down in the wood at seven o'clock on a summer evening for an hour or two of rest before the start of their late-night roaming across the golf course and the marshes up to Warton Crag.

It may have been the moon's influence that kept the roe deer from repose and me awake. I felt I could write things down; my mind was full of thoughts as bright as the moonlight, as often happens with people who can't sleep, and I remembered the poem by Ted Hughes called *The Thought Fox,* which I once saw him read and then explain as an idea entering the mind in one of those midnight moments on catching sight of a fox outside.

But then, in this moment of illumination, the big, shining moon became obscured by cloud again, the deer vanished and my bright ideas fled in sympathy.

February

1 February

Rain lashing against the windows at first light. Wind moaning in the trees. A trio of woodpigeons sitting motionless in the wood and a bedraggled pheasant trudging across a sodden lawn, having waited for the morning dole of grain which was late in coming. February Fill Dyke has arrived in a manner appropriate to its old nickname. The Anglo-Saxons called this the Sun-Month, the time when days began to lengthen and the sun began to show itself a little more. Not much sign of that today. They also called it Sprout-Kale, i.e. the cabbage month, when those necessary vegetables began to increase their growth. If yearning for the sun seems to be a lost cause for the time being, we can certainly look forward to the showing-forth of new growth very soon.

In the meantime, we have the never-ending rain as a diversion, as well as an inconvenience, perhaps. After a while it ceases to be an irritant and becomes a thing of fascination. I have been watching Hawes Water spreading into a field beyond its reedbed, reclaiming its old territory, as if yearning to meet the sea again, as no doubt it once did. The sea is making every effort on its part to bring about the reunion, with a high tide, heavy rain and strong winds combining to push the boundaries of Morecambe Bay right back to the Quicksand Pool Bridge, where I saw water flowing upstream in the ditches. Everywhere fields are flooded, particularly around Warton, which huddles against the Crag that dominates it and bears its name. Right now the village stands as if with its feet in the water and looks as though it ought to be renamed Waterton. Like Avalon in the old legends it seems to rise up from a mysterious lake and be in another world, not one in which people sit hunched over their computers or are glued to their mobile telephones. The rain showed no sign of abating, or the water of going down, and the winds roared all day, as if February, not March, were meant to come in like a lion.

3 February
The high wind continues. At Leighton Moss it did more than ruffle the waters, it sent waves scurrying across the pool and hurled itinerant gulls across the sky like scraps of white paper. The extensive reedbeds bent beneath the blast and if any bird lifted itself above the reed-tops, the wind took it. A heron took flight but was soon grounded again, and a brace of teal sprang into the air to head seawards but found themselves flung like arrows up the valley. A flock of ten greylags came from the north and glided quickly down towards the turbulent water, skimming along only inches from the surface but deciding not to come down in the mere. As soon as they lifted to clear the reeds again, their tight and purposeful formation was broken and the individual geese buffeted into wildly changing patterns of flight. The only birds which seemed to be enjoying the weather were a pair of buzzards, masters of the air as always and daring the wind to do its worst as they circled, almost danced round one another, a hundred feet up in an early nuptial display.

All of the other birds had their feet firmly on the ground today, or close to it. Most of the ducks were keeping out of the water, resting with their heads under their wings along the reedy edges: strongly marked shoveler, colourful teal, sturdy mallard and the rest. Unobtrusive gadwall sculled quietly under the shelter of the wind-whipped reeds. Only the tufted ducks ventured out into the open water, but being diving ducks they spent as much time under the waves as riding on top of them. Conditions were not ideal for bird watching even when the sun came out from behind the scudding clouds, but no matter. As so often happens when I visit the Moss, I found myself absorbed in the splendid landscape, the bowl of hills or high ground brimming with life and colour, even at this time of year. The steel blue of the water and the golden brown of the reeds complement perfectly the purple, cushion-like woods and the vivid green fields clothing the long western flank of Warton Crag.

Though most of the birds were keeping their heads down, the Moss was being visited by a numerous and colourful species this Sunday afternoon. Birdwatchers by the carload and the coach load had descended, many wearing the bright garb beloved of the outdoor clothing trade, the winter sports enthusiast and the casual country goer alike. Like flocks of gaudy birds, more exotic than the creatures they had come to watch, they perched in the sun on the benches around the car park, displaying traditional feeding habits: eating sandwiches out of plastic boxes.

4 February

Light began to grow soon after seven, but dawn broke exactly half an hour after, a splendid affair of rose pink streaked with blue. As always it was short lived, and gave way to a uniform dull grey. At least there were no shrieking gales 'blowing the earth up' as my grandparents used to say, and no driving rain either. With the absence of these tiresome distractions it was possible to listen to the birds singing, and to admire the snowdrops, which suddenly are everywhere in gardens, hedgerows and odd corners. The air had that almost supernatural stillness that follows a storm, and it was such a relief to walk in the quiet of the morning, but then, suddenly, round a bend in the lane, I came upon a rabbit crouching still as a stone towards the side of the road. Young rabbits are frequently met with in the lanes, where they innocently nibble the roadside turf only inches from the wheels of the traffic until they learn the hardest lesson of all. Yet if a full grown rabbit sits hunched and motionless in the road in broad daylight, it means only one thing, myxomatosis, that horrible disease which leaves the victim with a scarred face, a disease ridden body and, finally, utter immobility before death. Another time I would have put the wretched creature out of its misery, but I had my dogs with me and they of course were showing great interest, so I tugged at their leads and we walked on. The illness looked in its final stages; the rabbit would be unlikely to outlast the day.

This was the only sombre moment in an otherwise tranquil morning. Silverdale was an oasis of calm while elsewhere there were various manifestations of nuisance and danger: rising floodwaters, a lorry which had caught fire on the motorway near Carnforth causing huge traffic jams on the local roads, and an unexploded bomb washed up on the shore at Morecambe. The only event of any importance in our remote corner of a quiet village was the appearance of a stranger in the lane, in the shape of a domestic goose, a modern-day Jemima Puddleduck gone a-wandering and lost her way. A passing motorist shooed her into our garden. It's surprising how ready people are to do acts of kindness by handing problems on to others. Our visitor has stayed all day, following me about whenever I went out of doors, and as I fed her and spoke kindly to her she made herself at home and has every appearance of planning to remain here.

5 February

The tame goose was still there this morning, so I exerted myself and found her a home elsewhere, with other farmyard geese in a free-ranging flock.

7 February

The rain continues, and though it isn't really never-ending, it seems so. Everyone who doesn't have to venture out stays decidedly under cover, including the creatures in the wild. Only the water birds were active, such as the curlews in the field by the level crossing probing the rain-soaked turf with their long, curved bills. A single oystercatcher accompanied them, boldly black and white with bill and feet of striking orange next the discreet grey brown of his companions. A group of dunlin stood at rest with their heads beneath their wings, little dark shapes against the silver floodwater looking like so many fishing floats. Then they took off in a close-knit flock, weaving, twisting and darting across the shallow pools and over the reeds.

13 February

After many more days of wind and rain we had a calm, still, mild day, so mild that a blackbird sang, not a few tentative warbling notes as a trial before the start of the singing season, but a full-blown song, suddenly bringing a hint of spring to the still-wintry landscape. Such a beautiful, full-throated song, thought by many folk the finest birdsong there is and so evocative of an English spring. No wonder English settlers in the nineteenth century took familiar songbirds with them to their new homes on the other side of the world, as an ever-present reminder of the land they had left behind forever. I have heard the song of the blackbird in New Zealand, fluting and dream-like among the tree ferns and other exotic shrubbery, and the sound of it took my heart home instantly. The tree ferns are native there; the blackbird is the exotic. Here at home the blackbird's song seems the perfect sound for summer gardens, for the long, hot days of July and August, but that is to see the song from a human perspective, of course. By the summer the birds have largely fallen silent. There is no longer any need to defend territory as food is plentiful and the young have flown. Blackbirds have quite a short singing season, from March to May, with a little overlap in February and June, so we have to make the most of it. Happily the louder though less melodious song of the song thrush can be heard all year, and though the species is now sadly quite rare in parts of the country, it is still with us in Silverdale. We often listen to one pouring forth his song from a cherry or an oak near to the house.

14 February

Colder but still sunny and dry. More birds joining in the singing today, including chaffinch, robin, wren and woodpigeon, almost as if they do take some notice of the old country tale that the birds all do their courting on Saint Valentine's Day. Perhaps the new moon is encouraging their activity. It rose at six o'clock, just as the sun was setting. An impressionistic picture of grey-blue with a salmon wash overlaid with inky daubs of cloud.

Cedric and Hetty

15 February

A soft, misty morning, exquisitely calm and still, the only sound a robin's song, the essence of melancholy, a thread of silver woven into the grey velvet of the day. Cedric, our resident cock pheasant, who never strays farther than a field's length away from the garden, sat on the apex of the tool shed roof, monarch of all he surveyed but not caring to move, as pheasants do on foggy days in October and November. However this was no autumn day. Banks of snowdrops stretched all the way up The Row, and jasmine flowered round cottage doors like patches of pale sunshine. Crocuses are flowering in my garden. Blue tits are investigating each one in turn of the four nest boxes I have put up in the garden, and we hope to have them nesting in at least one, though there are plenty of places for small birds to nest in the cracks and ledges of the rocks and in the holes in the dry stone walls, if anything ever will be dry again after all the rain we have been having this month.

Actually the water levels have gone down in the fields, and at Barrow Scout Fields at the foot of Warton Crag there were lines of flotsam lying across the grass, where a dozen or so coot were feeding out of the water. Some large shallow pools remain, where redshank waded or flicked about in a sort of dancing flight, showing their white wing chevrons. A couple of hundred lapwings flew down and alighted, dominating the grassy field.

16 February

Our garden is full of rocky outcrops and the soil is thin, preventing the development of a vegetable garden, flower borders or any hard work of that sort, partly to my regret and partly my relief. Oak trees, ash trees and others

19

clutch the limestone pavement with gnarled and grasping roots. Mole hills are a great rarity, there being not enough depth of soil to give the moles sufficient encouragement in founding a colony. As for rabbits, I have only ever seen one in the garden, a buck which passed part of the winter under the tool shed, but left in the spring to try his luck elsewhere, where he wouldn't get a headache from the density of rock so near the surface.

The smaller creatures get by where others can't. The voles and the wood mice find enough space for their dens in all this rocky landscape, slow worms spend the winter hidden in holes, and the small birds find opportunites in the cracks and crevices. A natural rockery rears up behind the house, rising to second floor level, consisting of big limestone boulders which are lozenge-shaped like the snouts of small dinosaurs, scarred and fissured by frost, heat and water over thousands of years. Into the runnels and pockmarks a busy wren was poking his tiny but inquisitive beak, scurrying brown and mouse-like over the rocks and sometimes disappearing from sight altogether into some deeper crevice. He often searches for insect food in these places, but now he is also starting to look for somewhere to build a nest, a search which for a wren is no small undertaking as the cock builds several nests in sequence, the so-called 'cock nests', one of which his mate at last chooses as the nursery for her eggs.

Red Bridge Wood

Just above the wren's restless investigations among the crevices, a cock blackbird sat quietly meditating on a thick layer of moss on a flat-topped rock, like any gardener proud of his little patch of ground. Moss is an important part of the fabric of the nests of many birds, and will be much in demand soon. It is also a very good place to find food in the depths of winter or indeed at any time of year, as blackbirds know well, flinging it about quite carelessly, as they do the layers of dead leaves, but this morning our bird was content to remain in proprietorial fashion on his lawn of green moss. His spring plumage is already of the finest, faultless, uniform sooty black with a beak of crocus-yellow.

In the overhanging bushes blue tits were as busy as the wren, engaged in similar pursuits, picking tiny prey off the hazel twigs. Two cocks were competing for the attention of one hen, then going off to check the nest boxes again. All this bird-activity on view just by looking out of the window.

17 February

This is the last month of winter, very changeable with fine days punctuating a narrative of boisterous weather. Many birds are still visiting the tables for the food I put out, including newcomers, an infallible sign every year of imminent seasonal change. This morning a pair of greenfinches arrived, the first I have seen in the garden for months. Whereas chaffinches are in the garden all year round, greenfinches only come now after a prolonged absence, during which they have probably been not far away feeding in the woods and fields. They will stay to breed in our garden or the ones nearby, and are a welcome sight in their plumage of soft olive green with bright yellow patches on tail and wings.

19 February

A walk along Ford Lane to Waterslack, and down the straight, muddy track that leads to – nowhere. The cart track is riddled with pot-holes, each one full of clear water and bearing the long-toed footprints of a moorhen in the muddy bottom. A sluggish stream flows in the bottom of the steep-sided straight ditch that follows the straight track. It contains just a few strands of waterweed, no other life apparent. It runs alongside the level fields of Silverdale Moss, which in recent times has been farmed but long ago was swamp like the other Mosses in the area. The waterlogged fields are liberally furnished with clumps of rush, looking like brush-heads stuck in the peaty soil. The land has been drained in the past and is intersected by straight-ruled ditches needing regular attention to keep the fields in production. At the best of times this is a damp place, better suited to the cultivation of herons, eels and snipe than sheep or cattle. Indeed the land has recently been acquired by the R.S.P.B., and like the fields at Crag Foot will return to an uncultivated state. They are deserted now of all farm beasts, and the bleating of sheep comes down off the higher ground, from the sloping pasture under the eroded eastern flank of Arnside Knott, below the purple feathering of birch and the dark blotches of yew. They are farther off than they sound. At this distance they seem no bigger than white turnips put out for beasts to feed on, but the round, white shapes are moving.

A tractor starts up in a field, muck-spreading near the Knott. The muck is spread with a nauseating efficiency these days by the slurry-spray method. A train rattles along the valley, just a few yards from the rutted track. Two straight roads, representative of different outlooks, different eras. A car moves along the road on the side of the Knott. A jet war plane splits the sky asunder as it flies along the coast, well below the summits of the local hills. These noises jar they are an intrusion of the machine world in this older, more primitive place, but they are soon gone. Like so much else, a perception of this place depends upon disposition, mood and circumstances. It might seem forlorn, especially in its present state, but some of the passengers on the train might have had the chance to see the antiquity of the landscape, the ice-age scoopings and gougings, the shaping of a land far older even than the agriculture that has occupied it for such a relatively brief time.

The railway travellers will soon have been whisked on, and their attention with it, to the much more dramatic scenery of the Kent Estuary, the Bay and the beginnings of the Lakeland hills. The quiet comes back, and I am left unmoved by the contraptions of modern transport, standing at the end of the Nowhere Track looking up the narrow, round-bottomed, steep-sided valley between the Knott and Middlebarrow, where the tall and ancient ruin of Arnside Tower broods on its knoll at the dark edge of the wood. Its commanding presence impresses anyone who sees it for the first time with the sombre thought that this quaint, tumble-down building was once the only safe refuge in times of trouble in the dale, when violent men from the north came by sea to steal what they could and destroy the rest.

Otherwise it is not one of the more scenic local walks. It is not, so far, part of one of those interminable treks which are so popular these days with long-distance walkers, who are inventing more all the time. Nor is it part of any circular walk beloved of afternoon strollers. It is just there and back again. Even though the way was wet and muddy and the fields seemed deserted, there were golden tassels of hazel catkins dangling in the bare bushes. Though there are still no leaves on the trees, their sap is rising already, the green pulse of all living things is quickening.

The birds seemed to think so. As I turned and retraced my steps the 'pink' of chaffinches resounded in the woods, as if they were telling one another what their favourite feather-colour was. A song thrush sang loudly and somewhere a pheasant made occasional but determined territorial claims. A nuthatch attempted to raise the pitch and tempo of the concert, but the gentle song of hedge sparrow and the blackbird's warble maintained an even melody. High above, using the rising currents of air, a trio of buzzards floated effortlessly, birds utterly at home in the air. With sights such as these who needs to fly to the tropics or even queue to get in to the Lake District? This lonely little track is a Track to Somewhere after all!

21 February
Intermittent showers, getting heavier in the afternoon, leaving just a few gaps in which the birds could make themselves heard, including a wood-

pecker drumming somewhere in my wood and, particularly, a song thrush pouring out his song from the oak tree just in front of the house. A reed bunting turned up today for the first time this winter. It breeds in the local reedbeds and waterside vegetation, especially at Leighton Moss, but after the breeding season it moves to drier ground not far away and lives on seeds for much of the time. They have been coming to our garden in the late winter, presumably when food is hard to find elsewhere, but they certainly make their presence felt, squaring up to the other birds such as the chaffinches which are with us all year round. By and large the other birds perch on the edge of the table, or stand near the edge and peck cautiously, ready for flight at the slightest threat. The reed bunting's method is to occupy the middle of the table and feed steadily, flattening itself stubbornly when another bird alights and presenting a gaping beak and glaring a warning at any challenger, such as the nuthatch which tried a little intimidation this morning.

23 February
My son who lives in Kent tells me the daffodils are in bloom there and the flowering currant. A milder prospect to look forward to, because here we have only continued wind and, this morning, snow when we woke up with showers of hail and sleet during the day.

24 February
Walking in Eaves Wood. The weather had improved from yesterday and the sun was out, but the footpaths are very muddy after all the recent rain and even though there was a drying wind it sighed apologetically in the tree tops, as if regretful that it couldn't get down to help at ground level. Apart from this breeze there wasn't a sound in the wood, not a birdcall to go with the sunshine and brighten the afternoon. Hardly a bird to be seen, only a nuthatch appearing fleetingly and a robin which flitted beside me while I walked along the path, as if hoping I would disturb one of the big ant hills with my stick and wake any sleeping residents for his benefit. Teeming with life in the summer months, every ant heap is a desolate place now, a scene of loneliness and devastation littered with the remains of last year's endeavours. Each twig, stick and stem at least twice as long as the insect which carried it, lying in disorder like the beams, baulks and spars of a ruined city.

26 February
Everyone grows tired of this prolonged season of gales. Two months rain have fallen, or to be more precise have been lashed at us, in two weeks we are told. It certainly feels like it. The floods continue.

There are calm days though, and the sun shows itself now and then. It made valiant efforts today, breaking through towering white masses of cumulous cloud which billowed into a whole circus of fantastic shapes: trumpeting elephants, galloping horses and flying tigers.

Like the sun our daffodils are only thin gleams of yellow, straining in their green sheaths and waiting for the sun's rays to warm them a little more. We shall have to wait a little longer for their appearance, which is one of nature's commonest yet still one of the finest, still liable to move people to outbursts of Wordsworthian enthusiasm.

Another common but impressive sight, if you are in the right place such as the middle of a great city or, like me, in the middle of a swampy valley full of reedbeds, is that of the starlings coming home to roost. They come flying in at dusk to Leighton Moss, arriving sometimes singly, sometimes in twos and threes, more often in dozens, scores and even hundreds, merging into vast flocks of forty or fifty thousand to sweep across the reeds and fields, swirling like clouds of wind-driven smoke. This commonest of birds provides one of the most spectacular sights of nature to be seen anywhere, and tonight I watched the spectacle from Storrs Lane as the thousands upon thousands of tiny, dark, bullet-shapes all moved in unison across land and water, with a faultless precision no choreographer would ever be able to achieve with a troupe of dancers. Their only accompaniment was the booming of a bittern that carried across the valley. They ceased to seem like the chirpy little street-urchin birds we are so familiar with in backyards, on housetops or crowding the ledges of some great building in the city, and took on a collective grandeur, behaving as one entity, as if one mind controlled the immense flocks. All turned, twisted, soared and dived at the same time, or undulated in strange, broad waves that changed shape constantly but remained intact. Now and then there was a split in the vast flock and contingents of many hundreds broke away, but always they re-joined the main body, which from where I was standing began to assume a slightly surreal appearance as it surged across the valley time and again: a smudge, a thumbprint, a pattern of iron filings against the dark blue sugar paper of the sky.

Finally the starlings came close enough for me to be able to pick out individuals. They peeled off in droves from the main flock and dropped quickly into the reeds in an orderly fashion, like an army making camp for the night, each bird finding itself a reed stem to grasp, each bird twittering, whistling and wheezing its contribution to the gigantic night-song of its kind. This immense noise is no choral beauty, no symbol on earth of the choirs of heaven, but it is impressive, like the flocks themselves, because of its sheer volume, and at a distance it can sound like the whispering of the wind or the sighing of the sea.

Then, just as the flocks seemed settled for the night, the birds erupted from the reeds in a giant cloud and circled the darkening valley once more before coming down for the last time, finding a perch for the night and subsiding into immobility and silence.

March

1 March

The Month of the Mad March Hare. One of them comes into our garden at various times of the year but always moves in a sane and sedate manner at the back of the house where we can watch it from the windows. It is now that they take themselves off to open pastures and hillsides to cavort and leap in that curious way that has had humans baffled and intrigued for centuries and given rise to so much myth and speculation. I have seen them at their games in a field on the south flank of Warton Crag, a trio of hares leaping about and playing follow-my-leader in serpentine dances and figures of eight. No hares today, though something just as madcap. The lapwings have already begun their squealing and tumbling out of the sky down on the marshes. Never did courtship look so exuberant as this. Much more restrained but no less intense is the relationship of the pair of collared doves on the bird table, pecking alternately like the wooden chickens on the child's toy which bob up and down for invisible corn when the bat on which they are fixed is rotated and the swinging ball underneath pulls their strings. They always remain close together, a loving couple, like their cousins, the turtle doves, but unlike them a vigorous species expanding its range whenever possible.

Sixty years ago there were no collared doves in Britain, now it is one of the commonest garden birds in town or country. The first birds appeared in Britain in about 1955, with the first pair breeding in these parts at Leighton

Moss in 1964. This gentle, delicate-looking dove with its plumage of soft pinkish-grey hardly looks robust enough to have begun an epic colonisation of Western Europe, starting in the Balkans in the 1930s, spreading rapidly and eventually reaching as far as Iceland within about fifty years. It is one of the most remarkable stories of animal movements known to man. It is also one of the rare instances of a species thriving and increasing in the twentieth century, at a time when so many others suffered persecution and catastrophic decline, sometimes to the point of extinction. This sudden spread of the collared dove took place without intentional help from humans, though the feeding of livestock, especially poultry, seems to have made a large contribution. Another factor has been the long breeding season, which begins in March or even February, and lasts until October, enabling the rearing of five or even six broods if the conditions are right. The nest is a thin, flimsy-looking platform like that of other doves and pigeons, but sufficiently well built to support the two eggs and then the growing chicks. The pair have a strong and lasting bond, which is another factor in their success. Fidelity and hard work: the old nature writers would have made this bird one of the most praised creatures in the medieval bestiaries, those books of moral observation which purported to be natural history.

Our pheasant, Cedric, is ready for a mate, in fact three or four, because unlike doves, pheasants are polygamous. He struts about, crowing and re-establishing his breeding ground, and will be clearly wanting the place to himself soon. For the time being one or two other cocks come in to the garden to take advantage of the food we put out, but their days are numbered. Cedric is already practising fluffing up his feathers, until he resembles from the front a very large, round plum pudding, a rich, shining, brandy colour with black spots like currants. To go along with this bit of splendour there is his iridescent bottle green neck with its purple sheen, his ear-like tufts of head feathers and his broad collar or neck-ring, as white as the ruff of an Elizabethan courtier. His countenance is imposing, with large facial adornments of a geranium red and the ivory beak with its aristocratic curve. The picture is completed by his gold-streaked wings, his fine, long barred tail, and his claret-coloured lower back, which is the feature that distinguishes him most of all from the other cock pheasants in the neighbourhood. He is also larger than any of his neighbours, and shows that he means to carry on, after three years now, being Lord of the Manor of Red Bridge.

3 March

Perfect peace at Leighton Moss, not even many birdwatchers about. The screeching hordes of black-headed gulls are not back yet to plague the other birds, so the geese and ducks swim serenely on the placid meres. Greylags are much in evidence, and some Canada geese. Most of the male ducks are in fine breeding plumage, a teal drake in particular swimming very close to the hide as if keen to show off his handsome head of rich chestnut with large eyepatches of emerald green ringed with white. Wigeon look handsome with their chestnut heads and foreheads of old gold. Shoveler drakes, over and above the instant appeal of the spade-like bill which gives the species its name, are dresssed in plumage of black and white, light blue, bottle green and warm brown. The tufted ducks, in their bold array of black and white, wear their crests as proudly as a knight in a jousting tournament. Many of the drakes in fact are jousting just now, fighting over females or in territorial disputes.

I was half expecting the coots to join in as well, for they are among the more pugnacious water birds, and it is a common sight to see them chasing one another across the mere then fall to with flying feet and thrashing wings, flinging water droplets into the air. They are ready to confront other species, too, and the coot is the only bird I have seen respond in like manner when a black-headed gull was being even more of a bully than usual. Today, though, there were no coot-skirmishes, all of them behaving impeccably and sculling about mildly as if they were the most sober citizens imaginable, dressed in restrained black with just a hint of the dandy in the lobed green feet, the white frontal shield and the finely-pointed beak a delicate shade of pink.

Out of the water the coot's cousin, the moorhen lifted its long-toed green feet fastidiously as it stepped across the muddy margin. Also a dark-plumaged bird, it shows a little more variation in colour with its head shield of a bright red, its red beak with a yellow tip, and its white wavy line along the body – a sort of plimsoll line still visible when the bird slips into the water like a vessel launched effortlessly.

Also at the water's edge, back to back like bookends, a pair of snipe stood motionless and almost hidden among the low vegetation because of their plumage which is the colour of dead bracken and old reed. Last year's reeds themselves stand like ripe corn at harvest, acres of tall yellow stems protecting the new growth and much else besides. In the old days the reed was harvested for thatching, and made better roof-cover than wheat straw because it had grown with its feet in the water and, as a consequence, was good at keeping the rain out. Its seeds are an important source of food for the bearded tits which make a home on the Moss, and for mice and frogs besides, which in their turn are food for bitterns, owls and herons. So many living things are inter-dependent; it is only Man who tries to live apart without taking much heed of nature around him. Some of us try to cross the divide as best we can and find a way of helping, encouraging, even communicating with wildlife.

On the subject of which, it is said that you can attract various species of bird, such as bearded tit and water rail, by kissing your hand to them, or at least by sucking the skin on the back of your hand to produce a sort of cross between a kissing sound and a squeal. I'd never tried it before, but did so now and immediately struck up a conversation with a water rail which went on for some minutes. Unfortunately I couldn't understand what he was telling me, and my attempts at communication in his language must have taken an unfortunate turn and given offence, because after a while he broke off the dialogue abruptly. Another bridge between the species collapsing when half built.

5 March
The sun is stronger, warming the woodland floor. The absence of leaves makes the patches of sunlight all the bigger. There are heart-shaped celandine leaves everywhere, but only one flower as yet. In the garden the first butterfly of the season appeared, a peacock resting with its wings open on the weathered grey of a stone wall.

7 March
Walked up to Bank Well, one of Silverdale's many 'wells' or natural springs, around which the first clusters of dwellings appeared, giving the village the scattered, open appearance it still enjoys today. I went to see if I could find any frogspawn, but there was none to be seen, though I know it has been present in garden ponds locally for some time. It's hardly surprising I didn't find any: there were five pairs of mallard swimming in the small pond, and they will have been helping themselves to the spawn and any tadpoles which survived. Though when I saw them the five couples were enjoying an innocent honeymoon promenade in the lane, heedless of any traffic that passed by.

11 March
I went up to Warton Quarry, to see if the shelducks still gather there, as they have done for many years past, three or four pairs of them in a gathering before breeding takes place, but perhaps I am late this year because there are none to be seen. Now and then they have bred on the rock ledges, their tiny ducklings tumbling thirty feet or so when they left the nest and taking no harm at all when they landed on the tumbled mass of jagged rocks at the bottom of the cliff. It may be that the shelducks have thought better of the quarry as a nest site since the peregrine falcons came, but the peregrines need all the encouragement they can get, as a much persecuted species in the past, one suffering greatly from pesticide poisoning in the post-war years and still vulnerable from illegal trapping for falconry. The female sat at rest on a high ledge, just the sort of scene beloved of that greatest of bird artists, Charles Tunnicliffe: a plump falcon surrounded by the bleached and brittle stems of last year's valerian, like the bones of a pigeon carcase from some old kill. When she took wing the surrounding jackdaws sat silently in the trees around the quarry, where they still nest in the numerous crevices in the rock. They and their young are safe enough inside the limestone cracks, and it takes more than the loss of a few of their number during the course of the season to deter them from keeping to their well-established rock-face colony.

The afternoon was mild with a westerly breeze blowing away from the house, so I set about building a garden fire, to burn some of the brash left over from the woodcutting in January. It was still a bank of twigs as big and dense as a hurdle in the Grand National, in which a blackbird could well build its nest, misguidedly expecting green shoots to break out and hide the nest from predators. I have seen it happen before, so this pile of brushwood needed burning quickly.

There is something satisfying about constructing a successful garden fire, especially as they don't always catch first time and have to be rebuilt. It is almost as if they have a mind of their own. Curling wraiths of smoke form an attachment to you and, dog-like, follow you about, no matter where you stand to avoid them and what direction the wind is blowing.

The wind dropped. The evening was mild and sweet, with daylight lasting until half past six. Cedric the pheasant wandered across the lawn to see what I was doing, then sauntered off into the wood to roost in one of the trees, cock-cocking as he went. A song thrush sang and then blackbirds took over from him; a peaceful scene with beautiful bird-music. This everyday scene, commonplace you might call it, is why so many people watch birds. It is every bit as good a reason for belonging to societies like the R.S.P.B. as the sight of a spectacular bird like the peregrine falcon.

13 March

This morning there was only a neat cone of hot ash and charcoal left from yesterday's fire. Only a phoenix could lay an egg in it now. It was a cloudy morning, and I thought it might rain, as a green woodpecker seemed to think as well, because he was calling in the woods all round for quite a long time. His clear, ringing chuckle in the greenwoods was in the past always taken as a sign of rain, hence one of his country names – the rainbird. But he and I were both wrong, and the day brightened. A few more celandines came out, and I saw that the small, wild daffodils at the edge of the wood were showing as well. A good many jaded snowdrops are lingering, like a ground mist that is reluctant to fade away. With the wildflowers also come the weeds, nettle shoots in particular, though they are a reminder that it's time to gather some to make nettle soup. Rendered down like spinach then drained, nettles make very good soup, green in colour and mildly pleasant in taste.

There are spotted leaves of lords and ladies, as well, and an armoury of spear-shaped bluebell leaves. In the wood the dog's mercury is spreading its cover across the ground, reddish buds of elder are breaking open, showing tiny green shoots within, and the upright leaves of wild honeysuckle are like green flames spreading along the woody stems in the shade of the trees. The sun came out and the birds were singing, and Cedric came to feed near the front door, bringing a hen pheasant with him, the first we have seen since the autumn. He is very attentive, walking round her and displaying his feathers on the side nearest to her by dropping his wing, raising his back feathers and making a sort of shining, many-coloured disc of himself. He has immense confidence in his ability to make an impression and no doubt this is the start of his spring courtship. In the meantime a pair of crows begin to investigate the wood with a view to breeding there again.

14 March
Roe deer in the garden. A buck, two does and last year's full-grown fawn all came out of the wood and across the lawn at a brisk trot, then passed down the drive, straight out of the front gates and along the lane to Eaves Wood a couple of hundred yards away. Their direction and their haste suggested they may have been disturbed on the golf course. Though there is plenty of cover for them locally, much of it is in the daytime busy with people either working or vigorously pursuing their leisure activities. Disturbance therefore must be commonplace. Alternatively, the close formation and disciplined trot may be early signs of territorial assertiveness from the buck.

17 March
At last we saw our March Hare this morning, running along the edge of a reedy field at Silverdale Moss. The reed bunting is still on the bird tables, still holding his own against chaffinches, collared doves, nuthatches and even robins. It is not the only one of its species, having been joined by two other males recently. No females have been anywhere near.

18 March
A blackbird began the dawn chorus in the wood at half-past five this morning, with a song thrush adding his clarion call half an hour later and sticking to his last all day long, rain or shine. The ringing notes of a wren echoed among the trees from time to time, always somehow one of the most combative and arresting of bird songs. The mellow song of a robin provided that autumnal undercurrent as a reminder of the transience of things, always to be heard softly in the background while the repetitive notes of a greenfinch spoke directly of the crude surge of new life everywhere, reinforced by the drumming of a great spotted woodpecker on a telegraph pole. Two men from some agency or other have been to tell me that two such poles on my property have been condemned as unfit for use, but as they were unable to get them out of the ground and couldn't find anywhere in the rocky ground to dig a hole for a replacement, they went away again, baffled. No doubt they will be back to dig more holes in the garden one day, but in the meantime the poles remain, looking as solid as ever to me. The woodpecker's drumming was a confirmation, just a test for hollowness and insect infestation, ceasing as soon as he was satisfied there wasn't any. He probably found the seasoned wood an ideal medium for the drumbeat of his own spring message.

There are now two hen pheasants keeping company with Cedric. I recognised both of them this morning as his most constant companions from last year, Hetty and Hatty, distinguishable because one is pale and the other dark. I went out to feed them and they both rushed towards me, ignoring my bull terrier Toby, though I hadn't seen them for five months. Cedric stands proudly over his two hens, often waiting until they have finished eating before beginning himself. Afterwards he sometimes expects a favour from one of them for leading them in such an easeful life. Then he will stand erect, stretch his neck and flap his wings briefly before crowing loudly to let the pheasant world know his whereabouts. After crowing he finally flaps more vigorously, with sufficient force to make him stagger backwards. The performance being over, the hens disappear into the undergrowth while Cedric stands guard about halfway down the drive, on the watch for intruders.

22 March

The black-headed gulls are back, in very fetching breeding plumage of bright white, soft grey, chocolate brown and scarlet. This morning they were screeching carelessly up the valley and past the garden, rather like those few local maniac drivers who treat the country lanes as a private racetrack. They are always on the lookout for something to eat and, being omnivorous will devour anything from daddy-long-legs and winged ants to eels, mice and even the unwary, newly fledged young of small birds. There are none of those about yet and mostly the gulls keep to their colony down at Leighton Moss. In any case the blue tits are safe in their nest box close to the front door, taking no notice of anything as they go in and out with nest material. Even so the peanut feeder is perhaps too close to the nest box and I shall have to think about moving it soon.

In the meantime there is still a need for feeding the birds, or so they seem to be telling me when I get up in the morning. Later there will be plenty of insects about feeding on the new leaves, in turn to be fed on by the birds, but as yet we only have the hawthorn buds opening, and I can enjoy watching a little longer the pair of nuthatches which visit the nut-feeder, gripping it with the same upside-down ease with which they descend a tree trunk. They have yellow-buff underparts and slate blue backs visible in wonderful detail at such close quarters. Its rounded, short-tailed shape is a common sight in the woods and gardens of Silverdale, yet when I first came to the district thirty years ago there were no nuthatches here. They have successfully established themselves only in recent years.

23 March

Found a blackbird's egg on the ground just in front of the house. Half an egg to be precise, not the smashed relic of some predator's raid, but a clean, empty shell from which a chick has safely hatched. A parent bird will have carried the discarded shell away from the nest, probably beyond our garden, to drop it where it will not attract attention to the hatchlings. So one pair of birds are already hatching young, while others, even of the same species, are still building their nests. It literally is the case of the early bird catching the worm, for though nests are more exposed now before the leaves are out, and there is less food for nestlings about than there will be in a few weeks, some thick cover is available in the evergreens, and what grubs and insects there are will be sufficient for the successful hatching going on.

In our own garden a pair of blackbirds have just finished building their nest, a neat, rounded sturdy structure of dried grasses as grey as the ledge on the stone wall on which it rests. In spite of its camouflage colour, it is horribly conspicuous, and if I can spot it so easily, so can any passing crow, cat or tree rat. The proud builders seem to have had second thoughts as well, because as soon as they finished their nest they forsook it and set about making another one. The hen blackbird gathers moss which she carries off · to the thick ivy crown on part of our garden wall, while the cock keeps a close watch on her movements, taking care that she is not observed by the prying eyes of predators. They need to be careful, for the crow couple in our wood have taken up residence again and have just finished their own nest, in the top of a sycamore right in the middle of the trees. The choice of tree is probably no coincidence: sycamores come into leaf before the other trees, and although the nest is quite visible just now, it will soon be hidden from the world.

24 March
The first primrose showed itself in the wood, the first blackthorn blossom has appeared and the spotted, oval leaves of lungwort are fully out, with flowers of a vivid blue-purple sometimes shading to pink. The birds continue their nest-making, and un-making in at least one case. From a bedroom window we watched a pair of marsh tits taking out old nest material by the beakful from the same site they occupied last year: a cleft in a limestone boulder immediately behind the house. Spurred on by the example of the birds I got to work in the garden myself and went to the lawnmower, an old, British-made machine which started first time in spite of having been out of doors all winter, lately without even its cover which vanished in last month's gales. I cut one of the big lawns, depositing the great volume of grass clippings in flat-topped mounds reminiscent of the iron-ore waste deposited on the marshes in the days of the old Carnforth Ironworks long ago and still remaining as a landmark, or sea-mark, or an eyesore, depending on your point of view. I distribute the clippings as unobtrusively as possible about the garden and wood, but it is always a problem with such an area of grass. 'Get some sheep' people tell me, 'or a goat!' I can't help thinking that would be replacing one small problem with several larger ones. Perhaps I should plant more trees. Anyway, it was good fun being whirled round on the old Westwood, which did sterling service at Leighton Hall for a number

of years before coming in its retirement to endure with much stoicism the rock-strewn ground at Red Bridge.

25 March

After drier weather, a damp morning. Two hen pheasants with wet feathers standing waiting in the soft spring rain for a charitable donation. Hetty sat on the log pile near the door and Hatty stood on the seat of our garden bench close by. Cedric, their lord, stood (in lordly fashion) on the cover of the septic tank in the middle of the lawn where he enjoys a good, all round view and can be continually on the watch for intruders at this crucial stage in the season. The hens fed eagerly, having soon to begin egg laying, brooding and chick minding. Even when they had finished Cedric only sauntered up slowly as if enjoying his morning stroll across his new-mown and freshly watered lawn. At other times he stands over his hens as they feed, inflating himself and walking round them in a circle, tilting his feathers like a round shield at an angle in their direction in his 'disc' display.

26 March

After yesterday's mist and rain, and the mild and sunny days before that, a sharp frost this morning. 'Sample weather' my grandfather used to call it. The sun came out later and took all the frost away, making the white lawn green again. Before that the deer were foraging in the wood and the birds were as eager to be at the food I put out as they were at the beginning of the year. There was an addition to our bird table this morning in the shape of the curiously named twite, a member of the finch family and a rare visitor, which leaves its moorland home in winter for coastal regions, and is probably on its way back to the breeding grounds a little further inland now.

27 March

The frosty air didn't stop a blackbird from starting up at five o'clock this morning, and a song thrush soon after. The sun came out and dealt swiftly with the frost, as yesterday, and the afternoon was magnificently sunny, though with a sharpness in the air, too. It is still something of a novelty to walk on ground that isn't wet, and an air of ease has come over the land at last. The blackbird continued to sing and the roebuck lay still in the midst of a green bed of bluebell leaves in a secluded corner of our quiet wood where the first violets are out and more primroses have come into flower. Hidden in a shrubby corner of the garden I found a cluster of primulas of a soft, sky blue. There are violets out in the wood, and a broad scattering of celandines on the lawn.

Good Friday

A procession of motor-drawn caravans passing the front gate, oblivious to the drumming of a great spotted woodpecker which is visible from our house as he hammers away on a dead tree trunk just a few yards along Ford Lane. He has a well-chosen, resonant sounding post this morning. On either side of our gate, as a sort of welcome and farewell, is a borage-like plant with large leaves like spear-blades and bright blue flowers with white middles like speedwell or forget-me-not, but flowering earlier. It has a mysterious, foreign-sounding name, too: the alkanet, which is said to derive from an Arabic word for henna. Introduced to England in the middle ages, the plant has long been grown for the red dye it yields. It always strikes me as odd that a plant with flowers of such a vivid colour should produce a dye of a completely opposite hue.

The colour of the moment is undoubtedly neither red nor blue, however, but green. A flush of green is spreading slowly along the hedges, while the spotted leaves of that curious plant, the lungwort, growing in one of my flower borders, are surrounded by another oddity, the wood spurge, a plant with a woody stem, rosettes of leaves and green, flower-like bracts.

Easter Day
More variety of colour in the garden today. The flowering currant is producing its pendant clusters of wine-red flowers and my dwarf azalea is also coming into flower. The variety known as 'bluebird', it thrives year after year in a big pot, and wouldn't do so well if I were to plant it out in the limy soil of the garden. A cock bullfinch appeared on the rocks just under the bedroom window, the first one I have seen in the garden for several months. He was dressed in the most formal of clerical grey, white and black, with also the most ecclesiastical of crimson fronts. He was feeding with the restraint of an ascetic on the remains of dock seeds, dried and flaky as rusty iron, and searching among the bramble sprays for any last shrivelled blackberries from last autumn.

Church was full this morning for the most important festival in the Christian calendar. In the pew in front were a family of father, mother, boy and grandfather. The old man was very frail, sitting hunched, with head bowed all the time, but clearly determined to follow the service. His daughter sat with her arm round him to prevent him slumping in his seat and took her jacket off to place it behind his wasted body to cushion it from the hardness of the oak pew. At last they decided to go before the end of the service, just before the congregation went up to the altar. I got up to open the door for them. 'Sorry about this' muttered the old man as he passed. 'It's all right, don't worry,' I said, adding, 'God bless you.' I closed the door after them. No sooner had I sat down again than a tortoiseshell butterfly rose suddenly from the now empty pew in front of me and quickly ascended towards the light of the nearest lancet window. Its feeble form battered at the glass ineffectually, just as the old man's soul fretted in the failing body, waiting to get out.

April

1 April

I clambered up on to the central spine, bank or hog's back of limestone rising up at the back of the house and running up the middle of my wood, and there I stood for a while, taking stock of things. The rock here is of the limestone pavement type found all round Morecambe Bay: fissures and runnels called grikes eaten into the stone over time by frost and the action of running water, defining the 'clints' of remaining rock which emerge from the ground cover in cubes, lozenges, curious parallelograms and all sorts of odd geometrical shapes known and unknown to man. These limestone slabs may be made up of the petrified remains of an unknowable multitude of tiny sea-creatures, but they resemble the bones of vast pre-historic animals, at the other end of the scale of size. At other times the rocks seem just a jumble, at best a conjectural arrangement of pieces of a particularly inscrutable jigsaw puzzle.

Resting on the top of the pavement is a large boulder, about five feet high and as many across, wearing a crown of ivy on the top. There are others scattered about the wood, deposited like playthings some ten thousand years ago by the last ice sheet to pass this way. Wrens nest in their holes and crevices and small mammals make their homes in the sheltered ground beneath. I lean against this fragment of ancient glacial upheaval and look around me. The rocky ground – the clints – are covered with moss and tendrils of ivy, the basic ground cover or lowest layer of the wood. In the grikes lies a humus of old leaf litter out of which grow the perpetual clusters of hart's tongue ferns, now renewing themselves and being joined by bluebell leaves and the abundant growth of dog's mercury. These plants and others like them still to come form the second layer of woodland growth, above which grows the underwood or third layer, of bushes of varying heights: hawthorn, holly, hazel, spindle and bird cherry, with, round the edges of the wood, the familiar shapes of elder, blackthorn and buckthorn, twined with thick woody stems of honeysuckle. This layer is dominated by the towering growths of mature trees, the oaks, ashes, wych elms, sycamores, cherries and small-leafed lime.

This richly-textured woodland consists in fact of more than four layers. Four suits the limited eye and the mathematical mind of the human observer. In reality a wood of some age which has not been interfered with too much is multi-layered, multi-dimensional, with intersecting planes and curves of activity where the birds and insects live. The curved line is greater than the straight one, as John Ruskin said and as true artists know, and thus in the inspired design and ornamentation of our great gothic cathedrals we see a representation of the flowing lines and soaring heights of our woods and forests.

4 April
There was a thick mist to begin with, and though there was also a strong light behind it as the sun tried to burn through it, there was a decided chill in the air, which carried the surrounding birdsong with exceptional clarity. The bird calls also had a new urgency about them, the ringing notes of a song thrush, the crowing of a pheasant, the caw of a black crow, the call of a great tit like the striking of a tiny anvil, even the cadences of hedge sparrow and chaffinch, all in a fever of courtship and nest-building, all urged on by the nuthatch cry of 'do it, do it!'

The sun broke through the dissolving mist and warmth stole over the valley. Ponies trotted skittishly in the field below Challan Hall and the rabbits came out of their warrens nearby to sit in the sun and nibble grass stalks. The bird song now was that of sunny weather: the cooing of a ring dove, the warbling of a blackbird, the wheezing of a greenfinch. I spent a hot afternoon in my garden, where the sun is bringing out more colour among the flowers, the white of bridal wreath and ruby red of flowering currant, for example. In the wood a roe deer lay at rest among the dog's mercury and bluebell leaves, avoiding both the heat and the human activity in the bigger woods, the local gardens and the golf course.

5 April
A hare came down the broad path in our wood, a few days too late to be a March Hare, unless he was working to the Old Calendar. There was new life apparent in my gnarled and weatherworn damson trees, white blossom

coming out before the new leaves. Blackthorn blossom is also coming out in my garden and along the lanes, where it rides along the hawthorn hedges like white wave crests on a green sea. There are hawthorn leaves of a vivid green out in my wood, too, where it forms a sort of green mist hovering a few feet off the ground.

Cedric the pheasant accompanied me on my morning walk round the wood, in front to begin with at a respectful distance from the dogs, then allowing me to pass him where the path narrowed when we were half way round. He followed me down to the house again and waited patiently for his breakfast. He spends a lot of time on guard, standing on a rock, a wall or a shed roof, vigilant against intruding males of his own species and on the watch for unattached females who might still be looking for a mate. During the last few days there have been numerous fights and the stormy courtship of a new hen which appeared but which played hard to get and, after a good deal of chasing, decided not to go ahead with the liaison after all and went away again.

The lambs in the fields all round us are growing well and turning into sturdy little creatures, but new ones are still arriving, spindle-legged and shaky, staying close to their mothers while those a week or two older frisk and race about in gangs just like children in an infants' school. Half a dozen of them were still racing about at half past eleven last night, long past their bedtime, with only the light from a street lamp on the corner to see by.

The evening was very sunny, and at half past six I went down to Leighton Moss to the sight I never tire of, the broad band of golden reed between blue water and the wooded hill of purplish-brown. I was greeted by the song of a blackcap, newly arrived from winter quarters probably, though in the past I've seen individuals in the garden that have braved our winters. A marsh harrier swept lazily across the reeds, back again after its spring migration, and sand martins passed repeatedly over the ruffled waters of the mere. Bitterns boomed. A sparrow hawk appeared, looking for his supper among the array of small birds around the Reserve, putting them all in a panic. All the above were brown birds, large and small, visible and invisible, but the dominant colours of the water birds were black and white: a pair of goldeneye, a quartet of Canada geese, boldly marked shelduck, argumentative black coot and silent, radiant white swans like galleons on a blue sea. The black-headed gulls form a brash, noisy, assertive colony of birds which are more marsh gulls than seagulls, perfectly at home in a place like the Moss. They are wrongly named, having heads which are not black at all but white in the winter and now, for the summer season, a handsome chocolate brown. The rest of their plumage is also strongly marked and appealing: pure white and soft grey, with bright red bill and legs. Oh, that noise! Still, it is one of the best birds for a beginner birdwatcher to sharpen his identification skills on and, as the more experienced and cynical ornithologists say, they are a plentiful source of food for marsh harriers, taking the pressure off the more vulnerable species.

7 April
The air was chill in the wood this morning, but the sun streamed through the trees throwing bars of light across the burgeoning plant life on the woodland floor. The clear air rang with the crisp drumming of a woodpecker, the constant refrain of a song thrush and the anvil-call of a great tit. A pheasant joined in from time to time. The countryside often isn't completely silent, though people who are town dwellers in fact or at heart somehow expect it to be and get irritable at the bleating of sheep, the crowing of a cock, the ringing of church bells or the barking of a deer. The sounds fit in, they blend, they seem right because they *are* right, including tractor noises and the sound of woodcutting. The tranquility comes from everything fitting together and forming a harmonious whole.

In the afternoon the air was warmer, and I took a walk across the fields to Challan Hall. Lambs stood among the ivy-leaved speedwell and the yellow celandines, innocently staring at me as I took the path across their pasture. They stood their ground because they were standing next to their mother, but on splayed legs not altogether under their control.

Heaps of sawdust and bark chippings edged the railway track, left behind after the recent tree-felling and clearing of scrub along the embankments, though it was good to see that bramble and blackthorn had been left because they posed no threat to trains or overhead power lines. Thus an important wildlife habitat has been preserved, where butterflies danced in the afternoon sunshine, colourful small tortoiseshells and showy peacocks, settling their delicate frames among the celandines or on the hot metal of the railway lines, such fragile, easily crushed creatures resting briefly on a symbol of man's perpetual restlessness and his hardness of purpose.

The stillness of the hot afternoon was broken at this point by a helicopter passing overhead, fortunately high up so that its noise was only a muffled roar. The machine flew heavily in a direct path, no erratic dance of a light frame, only the purposeful flight of whirling and uncompromising blades. Happily the passing of this flying machine did nothing to disturb the butterflies, or a pair of marsh harriers circling Hawes Water, a reddish male and a pale-headed, larger female which came and settled in a tree at the edge of the field I was in. Most likely she was keeping her eye on the rabbits that infest the rough pasture below Challan Hall. Rabbits may be an easier option than hunting prey in dense reedbeds, especially the young rabbits of this season which sit outside the warren quite boldly until danger threatens, which sometimes they don't see until it is too late. Some of them bolted into their burrows at my approach, but others sat on and watched me inquisitively as the lambs had done.

The woods around the Hall were full of primroses, violets and the flowers of wild strawberry, a sort of William Morris tapestry of flowers to add to the richness of new life all around. Somewhere in the woods a green woodpecker gave his laughing call and my progress down towards the lake was arrested by the behaviour of a pair of nuthatches on a sycamore, where the female was investigating a potential nest hole. The male kept attentively close by, giving the usual call but also a longer one, quite loud in his declaration of attachment, whilst opening his wings and displaying his chestnut flanks. High in a pine tree a chiffchaff was singing, a small, pale green warbler visible at last after being only a voice in the woods for several days.

I walked round the lake, noting where the footpath has been diverted and trees felled for the preservation of grassland on the margin and the protection of rare plants. Last season's bulrushes were bursting open like over-filled chocolate éclairs, spilling out their creamy masses of tiny seeds to drift on a freshening breeze. In Moss Lane the bees were buzzing in the blackthorn blossom and the pussy willows. Everywhere there is a burgeoning of flowers, a flurry of insects and the feverish activity of birds.

9 April

The warmer weather encourages this activity, though there are still some birds which are biding their time, as if reluctant to acknowledge the start of the breeding season, such as the trio of male reed buntings, which were joined this morning by two cock sparrows, a rare occurrence for this garden and an opportunity to compare the plumage of these two species which are sometimes mistaken for one another.

Other birds, though, are well into the swing of things, all at different stages of their breeding cycle, some with young already hatched, some with eggs, some still building and others only at the courting stage. Just now the chaffinches are at that point, in a sort of collective nuptial display, the males chasing one another all over the place in competition for the females which can hardly be said to be in short supply and wait about in apparent unconcern, presenting themselves with fluttering wings and raised tails to a successful suitor.

The most noteworthy sight, however, has been the opening of the daffodils, which have come into flower under the cherry, spindle and pine at the edge of the wood and now lie as a thick band of bright yellow, an emblem of the spring sunshine itself. There are many other flowers out, such as forget-me-not, little curled fists of buds opening into five-petalled blue flowers with white or yellow middles. Like many wild plants, it was once used as a herbal remedy and a good luck charm; now it merely charms the eye and is part of the great spring restorative after the rigours of winter. It is joined by wild strawberry, and by ground ivy, a resilient little creeping plant with horizontal, rooting stems and toothed leaves which are round or kidney shaped. The flowers are blue and tube-shaped. It used to be used in brewing long ago, before the introduction of hops. It is easy to overlook such a plant, and even if noticed it is likely to be regarded as a weed these days. Even if we have enough plant-knowledge to recognise it, and glory in the diversity and richness of living, growing things, we can hardly feel as people must have done in times long gone by, when the appearance of every living thing had some special significance, whether religious, social, medicinal or culinary.

These days, instead of searching the hedgerows for healing herbs, charms against the evil eye or plants to put in the stock-pot, we are more likely to see a warm spring day as a chance to get out into the garden and wage war against plants which we regard as having no right to be there, that is unless we drop everything and go for a walk, or head for the golf course. The warmer weather also means more people playing golf, for more hours each day, which is one of the reasons for the roe deer spending more time in our wood, using it as a haven or retreat. A family of four, the buck, two does and one fawn from last year have been resting there in the morning and evening, but are now starting to come down to the front of the house in the middle of the day. The ground rises up at the back of the house and on either side, and we often see them passing the window as we sit reading or watching television. Today the buck came to observe these armchair naturalists and stood right at the edge of the lawn where the rock falls abruptly to the level of the house, only three feet away from the window and so close we could see his eyelashes and the spring moult where his winter coat is falling away in patches. Without concern he stood above us, nibbling the grass and dandelions among the cascade of heather, aubretia, saxifrage, bellflower and tiny ferns.

11 April

As I came out of the house this morning a crow called out a loud 'caw' as if offering a greeting, and bowed to me very civilly several times from his vantage point in the top of a bare oak. More likely he was calling to his mate sitting on the nest they have been building together in the wood, a bulky inverted cone of sticks and twigs which is still perfectly visible as only a few trees are beginning to show any leaves. Nest-building can take up to three weeks, though my pair haven't taken that long, being old hands at the game and having a ready supply of materials close by. Incubation is supposed to be done by the female alone, but I distinctly saw a change-over take place later today, one crow leaving the nest and the other taking its place, probably to give the female some breathing space to take exercise and find food for herself, whilst not leaving the eggs vulnerable to predators such as magpies and, particularly, other crows which would speedily take advantage of an unguarded nest with eggs conspicuous without the protection of a canopy of leaves.

15 April

Four roe deer on the lawn, all looking rather 'moth-eaten'. At least one of the two does is pregnant. The yearling will most likely live separately from the others when the new births take place, indeed they will all lead more solitary lives for a few months. When they had gone I went out to gather some flowers for indoors, tall yellow daffodils and white narcissus. The shorter wild daffodils at the edge of the wood are already past their best, but these cultivated varieties are still going strong, forty yards of them all along one side of the drive. Half way along this row Cedric stood like a sentinel, not concealed but perhaps enhancing his status, using the bright flowers as a setting for his remarkable plumage. Who knows what distant origins our own love of colour and display has? Not very far away, also among the daffodils, another cock pheasant lay concealed, only breaking cover at the last second as I unwittingly stumbled upon his hiding place and plucked a flower just in front of his head. He gave me a start, and clearly Cedric hadn't known of his whereabouts, that an unwanted visitor was lying in wait for an unsuspecting hen to pass by when Cedric wasn't looking. Now, however, Cedric *was* looking, and set off in hot pursuit of the other bird, taking flight and chasing him over the garden wall, across the lane and into the fields towards Challan Hall, cock-cocking vehemently. The flurry and the noise subsided, and a brimstone butterfly rose silently like a detached flower and passed across the lawn.

In the calm of this fresh, sunny April morning a blackbird began to sing, that clear, fluting song of promise flowing from the cherry blossom which hangs cloud-like just by the house. The humming of bees drifted along with the song of the blackbird. In the wood the bluebells are starting to flower and there are violets, primroses and wood anemones, all favourite spring flowers and presently decorating the woodland floor with their blues and yellows. Less admired but just as welcome and equally fascinating is the cuckoo pint or wild arum, also known as lords and ladies, as well as a host of other country names, often to do with lovemaking because of the suggestive shape of the flower, a broad curving sheath of pale green (called the 'spathe') containing an upright, club-shaped purple flower-head (or 'spadix'). They bloom under trees and bushes, but are noticeable because of their size, colouring and distinctive shape which, along with the spotted leaves shaped like arrow-heads, are one of the great sights of April hedgerows.

Much less wellknown is the toothwort, a strange, ghostly plant growing in the wood just now. It has pale cream shoots and tight clusters of pink flowers, but unlike the cuckoo pint it has no leaves worth talking about, and creeps about feeding on the roots of hazels and other trees. It is parasitic it has no green colouring at all, which gives it a deathly pallor especially noticeable in the shaded places where it grows, giving rise to the old country name of 'corpse flower'. There was a belief that such a strange-looking plant could only be growing where a corpse lay buried in an unmarked grave. After some reflection I decided not to investigate the truth of the legend.

The trees themselves still have few leaves on them, though the wild honeysuckle continues to produce its erect, flame-like leaves burning with a green light where the climbing stems have twined themselves among the budding hawthorns and up the trunks of oak and ash. Opportunistic syca-more saplings are already in full leaf, taking advantage of the sunlight still shining strongly through the bare branches of the mature trees. It is the same in Eaves Wood, where I walked later on, though the buds of beech are swelling in preparation, thousands of them shining palely in the sun: a tree full of jewels better than any fashion mannequin dripping with diamonds.

In Eaves Wood the wood ants have emerged, thousands of them swarm-ing like football fans to a match dressed in their uniform of claret and black, but with more purpose, attending to the repair, consolidation and exten-sion of their colonies. I watched them covering an old tree stump which was worn to a shell and being used as a basis for the ant-citadel, to which unending cohorts brought fragments of stick and stem to add to the fine tilth of soil they had dug out to make their ramparts. Nowhere is there a better showing forth of the tremendous surge of spring energy manifesting itself everywhere just now, promising new growth, renewal and resurrection after the dead time.

16 April

If spring is an agreable time for gardeners, ramblers, naturalists and human observers of all sorts who feel secure enough to look at the world with detachment, it is a testing time for the wild things, a time when their eager-ness to reproduce and increase their kind is tested by constant checks and struggles. Even the pheasants, which come out of the woods and fields to feed half-tamely, half-warily in front of our very doors and windows, have their battles in this season of opportunity. Cedric our favourite defends his territory vigorously, two or three times a day, from envious rivals who covet his hens and his secure breeding ground of wood, field and garden. His glo-rious long, barred tail feathers were bent in some recent skirmish, and when I threw down a handful of corn for him this morning I saw that they were broken and trailing at a ridiculous angle.

He gives a chucking call, warmly like a barnyard fowl, as I approach him, as if he is reassuring and encouraging me rather than the other way round. Then when the seed is scattered his tone changes as he feeds, to a plain-tive squeak resembling the noise of a rusty gate, though uninterrupted by the feeding. Then he goes back on guard duty for the rest of the day. That doesn't stop other cock pheasants from creeping in unannounced, however. This morning a lame one suddenly appeared, having flown in unobserved, to try his luck at the feeding ground. One leg was crippled and utterly use-less, so that the bird had to proceed along the ground in a series of painful hops. Pheasants are curiously prone to this, perhaps because they are big birds and land heavily, or perhaps because of some arthritic tendency, a genetic fault brought about by captive breeding. They can survive for some time with the use of only one leg, so long as the power of flight is unimpaired, as Henry Williamson shows in his novel 'The Phasian Bird'. The stranger was chased away by Cedric of course, but he came back later, and in his turn chased away an able-bodied interloper, which he put to flight. Even in his distressed and makeshift existence he is unable to ignore the territorial urgings of his kind.

19 April

Feathery leaves are just sprouting on our ancient rowan, but the underwood or lower growth still shows the way, particularly the brilliant new hawthorn leaves hanging like a green haze everywhere. When I was a boy we used to pick these fresh green shoots, which we called 'bread and cheese', and eat them on the way to school, and the sight of the flush of hawthorn spreading along the hedges each spring is still to me one of the most heartening sights of the year.

It is one of those sights we come to depend on, another of those encouraging signs of renewal but with these openings and beginnings there are, always unexpectedly, the earliest signs of fruition and completion. The purplish flowers of the wych elm have given way to clusters of round, flat fruits, each one a notched, circular wing with a seed in the middle. They form before the leaves are out, a curious inversion of what we normally expect. They are already full size and will ripen and fall in July, months before the seeds of other trees. Indeed the wych elm spreads by means of its seed rather than sending suckers underground from the parent tree, and this has made it more resistant to Dutch Elm Disease. The timber is hard and water-repellant, and had many uses in joinery in the past, including boat building, the construction of water pipes and even coffin making. Small wonder then that this precocious surviver was regarded as a lucky tree and a charm against witches.

The flowers of the wild cherry also come out before the leaves, and mine are in full flower just now, cloud-like masses of white along the edge of the wood to add to the blackthorn which is still in bloom. The theme of white is continued on the woodland floor, where the windflower or wood anemone is out, delicate-looking flowers which tremble in the wind, though the plant is hardy and widespread. They are joined by the flowers of stitchwort, each with five forked petals growing with the narrow, grassy leaves on straggling stems which are easily snapped or pulled up, though unwisely according to folklore, because pulling up a stitchwort plant caused thunder and lightning.

None of that today, though. Just a mild day in mid-April with a deer at rest among the emerging bluebells and the butterflies settling where the celandines are thickly scattered in the clearing in the middle of the wood. The only sounds were of bees humming, the slow clop of horses' hooves in the lane and the song of a newly arrived willow warbler up in the trees. There is no place like a wood for feeling at peace with oneself and the world. This mystical mood continued into the evening, when in a cloudless sky a rare planetary display was to be seen, a diagonal alignment in the western sky of Jupiter, Saturn, Mars, the Crescent Moon, Venus and even Mercury showing itself above the horizon. A manifestation which the ancients would have regarded as auspicious but which we merely see as an astronomical curiosity.

20 April

Birdwatching down at the marshes, between Cotestones and Jenny Brown's Point. I'd gone to look for a little ringed plover that I'd heard about, but the rarity eluded me. Instead a lone oystercatcher piped a lament by the banks of the Keer, a veritable mud-snake of a river slithering its way over greasy looking sands between banks of grubby turf towards the Bay. As I trudged back along the hard, dusty track on the embankment between the river and the old rubbish tip the scene seemed a desolate one, but these acres of fields and marshland, though empty of people, are full of life, especially birdlife, from linnets singing in an elder tree to the swallows which suddenly came swooping in from the long journey from Africa, on exactly the same day as last year. Before following the river inland they paused to criss-cross the grass-covered site where rubble, garden refuse and broken household goods used to be tipped. Could any dull scene be better enlivened?

There was nothing dull about the pools close to the railway lines where ducks and waders were gathered in abundance. Restless, piping redshank probed the shallows and neat, compact dunlin stood at rest on one leg. Several pairs of shelduck swam in the brackish water in stately fashion or paraded on the banks like courting couples behaving with immense propriety and restraint. Unusually for ducks the sexes are much alike, both male and female having bright red bill and feet, dark green head and neck and white body with broad chestnut-coloured breast band. They are among the most colourful of our waterfowl, and always a delight to see. Their nesting is about to begin, but for now they are content to show off their fine plumage.

There were also eighteen black-tailed godwits in the pool, large waders with long straight bills for deep probing in the mud. They have only re-established themselves as breeding birds in Britain in the last fifty years, and visit this area on passage to their breeding grounds. Like many birds their numbers can be dramatically affected by changes in habitat, in this case by more intensive grazing, particularly by sheep, which reduces or removes suitable nesting sites in longer grass.

The godwits are a birdwatcher's treat, and their presence reminds us that Morecambe Bay contains the most important group of estuaries for waders in Great Britain, but even stronger proof is provided by the avocets, those leggy, black and white birds with upcurving bills which they sweep from side to side as they wade through the shallow water to capture tiny invertebrates. I watched a pair of them this morning on a little island in one of the lagoons. They are now established as a breeding species here. That this great rarity, the symbol of the R.S.P.B. no less, should be extending its breeding range northwards in England is a great thing, giving encouragement to conservationists to provide further suitable sites for this striking pied wader and to redouble efforts to encourage other rare birds to extend their range.

Saint George's Day.
It was still dark at a quarter past five this morning, but our cock pheasant crowed in the wood and that seemed to be the signal for the Dawn Chorus to begin because the blackbirds struck up at that moment, then a song thrush joined in almost immediately. Next came the tinkling bells of the blue tits, the metallic, repetitive call of a great tit and the brisk, busy song of the ever-active wren. The hedge sparrow and the robin wove their songs in discreetly, and each chaffinch round about threw his descant in for good measure. The cooing of doves, even the harsher sounds of a crow and a pheasant, punctuated the more melodic singing, but the swelling chorus of the blackbird melodies formed the heart of the performance. As this strong affirmation of imminent daybreak continued, a single owl hoot signalled that the night creatures were on their way to bed. At a quarter past five the air round the gable end of the house was thick with pipistrelle bats, milling about in a great congregation in a sort of communal aerial dance. They skimmed the eaves – and my head – with remarkable skill, speed and timing, just missing the solid walls or the sharp edges of the slates time and time again as they repeatedly approached their entrance holes then returned to the throng. They appeared to be enjoying the last few minutes of darkness rather than spreading out in search of flying insects as they had been doing all night. At last, one by one, these silent revellers made one last circuit and suddenly found themselves at their front door. Without fumbling for a latch key they clung briefly to the barge board and slipped in between it and the slates. By half past five they had nearly all gone in, and five minutes later there were none in the lightening sky.

Dawn came, and the chorus of birds ceased. Only Cedric continued to crow in the wood, standing on a mossy rock surrounded by bluebells, letting the world in general and other pheasants in particular know that here was a good piece of territory, with grass to forage in and woodland to nest and roost in, and he was lord of this peerless paradise.

Other birds were busy. Our three reed buntings have disappeared, after being with us for seven weeks, and have almost certainly flown down to the reedbeds at Hawes Water or Leighton Moss. Their place was taken this morning by a 'charm' of goldfinches, resplendent in their plumage of yellow, warm buff and crimson. They seemed like splinters of sunlight darting and fluttering across the lawns looking for dandelion heads already seeding. A chiffchaff began singing in an oak which is full of bran-coloured buds fat almost to bursting. Our resident crows, both of them, were off the nest and taking advantage of the ants which nest every year on the lawn. They spread their wings and tails and allowed the insects to travel up the feathers and eject formic acid onto both skin and feather, a sort of personal 'spring cleaning'. I have seen this 'anting' in all sorts of birds, including jays, blackbirds, starlings and woodpeckers. It is thought to be a stimulant to the skin, or else an insecticide or means of controlling feather lice and other parasites. Whatever its purpose, its practice is widespread and of obvious benefit, one might even say a source of enjoyment, to the practitioners!

26 April
The pheasant saga continues. Sidney has turned up, the youngest of last year's chicks and the only survivor of his particular brood. For a long time last summer he was literally at the bottom of the pecking order, and his heroic attempts to snatch food from the edge of the family party were met with frequent pecks from his half-siblings. Sidney, like the ugly duckling however, has survived to become an ornament to his tribe, a very handsome bird like his father, with a nice deep white collar, not quite so deep as Cedric's, and his tail coverts sage green instead of his father's wine red. I spoke to him, and he let me approach him, even though it is some months since I last saw him. He is mindful no doubt that I was a welcome source of food last year and likely to be so again. Cedric puts up with this most junior member of his family, giving him the 'disc' or 'plum pudding' display as the youngster feeds, whereas any other young cocks are given short shrift, especially Simon, the most assertive chick last season who still attempts to come into the garden and is always driven off by his father. Now, when Cedric decided his offspring had had enough, he escorted him off the premises, the gentlest I have ever seen him do it.

30 April
This has been a fine spring month, the air cool for much of the time with even a touch of frost now and then, but dry and sunny with new leaves and flowers bursting forth daily. April ends with rain, though. Our resident toad came out from the log pile where he has spent the winter and stood stiff-legged in the open with his body off the ground, looking as though he didn't know if he liked the rain or not. It's not common to see him in the light of day, though I often meet him in the evenings when he comes out to help himself to the abundance of slugs which it seems, prefer my garden to any other in the village. Perhaps I am to blame for his appearance, because we

are still having log fires in the evenings and the woodpile by the door is now very small, so the toad has been temporarily evicted, until I move the fresh-cut logs from the pyramid in the wood. At least the toad didn't come into the house to complain. In the past all sorts of errant and itinerant animals have made free with the inside of my home, not just the usual spiders – which are welcome – and flies – which are not – or the moths which blunder inevitably towards candles or light bulbs in the evening and the butterflies which come in through the open windows by day. If the front door is ever left ajar there is always the likelihood of an inquisitive toad or frog making its way indoors, especially in wet weather as if, contrary to all received opinion, they didn't like the wet. Once a swallow came in and couldn't find its way out again at first, and once a wren. Blue tits and robins often visit, and even a pheasant or two of the tamer sort, venturing into the porch where they have guessed we keep their food supply. We have the bats in the roof spaces of course, and sometimes one will come through an open window on a summer evening and flit before our unbelieving eyes as we sit watching television. Usually they go happily on their way, almost apologetically, when they discover their mistake, though now and then one takes a fancy to the place and we find it comfortably hanging in a curtain the next morning and have to remember to help it on its way the next night.

The pheasants stood bedraggled but stoical in the rain: Cedric, Sydney and Hatty, watching me as I went outside, as was Simon the interloper from his wall across the lane nearly a hundred yards away. Later he slipped into the garden and hid. He is a remarkably persistent bird, and very good at hiding. Pheasants are good at flattening themselves and can easily be lost to sight in grass of only two inches growth. I have seen them try the same trick on a shaven lawn when danger threatens, though then it doesn't work and they can be seen of course. Even so, a pheasant which crouches in this way is far less easy to pick off the ground, and it looks as though it is a defensive strategy evolved to protect against eagles and large hawks.

Simon isn't always seen by Cedric, but he was this morning, when he was set upon and put to flight, though he continued to creep back. Strange how one son is accepted calmly and the other is driven violently away. In the jostling for position which is going on between these two brothers, Sidney is in the lead quite clearly. Nevertheless the game of cat and mouse went on all day.

May

May Day

There are now broad swathes of bluebells brightening the wood, through which the roe deer picked their way this morning, coming down to graze on the lawns where cowslips grow in clusters of a luscious, butter-yellow. The deer take an exploratory nibble at these flowers now and then but by and large seem to leave them alone. The spring moult of all four deer continues and they all look moth-eaten. The buck in particular has shed a lot of his thick winter coat, so looks leaner than he did. A sleek, plump-looking jay eyed the roebuck with what appeared to be disdain: 'To be so skinny in such a time of plenty, sir! It's affected, it's positively perverse!'

Our cock pheasant, Cedric, turned up late this morning for his breakfast. In fact it was only ten minutes to noon when he finally put in his morning appearance, which seemed odd as he is usually waiting for a hand-out when we get up in the morning, but then I remembered that he fed so well last evening before going off to roost that he had probably not needed to stir himself to find food all morning. One of our fine black crows flew down from the nest in the wood behind the house to join Cedric, two large, glossy birds feeding side by side, one all black and one brilliantly coloured. Cedric took no notice of the newcomer, and it was in fact the crow which was ill at ease, circling the pheasant, stretching out his beak to grab at a seed or two at the edges of the scattering of grain then dancing away in case of trouble from a bird larger than himself and one with such self-possession and magnificent plumage. When the crow had gone Sidney came down to feed, and both he and Cedric trustingly took grain from the palm of my hand.

5 May

A blackbird started singing at a quarter to five this morning, well before daybreak. Sunlight touched the treetops of Eaves Wood and the heights of Slackhead, then streamed through our wood at six o'clock. It was a day of calm and quiet, with the air very still and cool. The cooing of doves and the soothing, fluting song of blackbirds were soft and gentle sounds enhancing the mood of the day. A whitethroat perched on a sloe bush, put up his crest and sang his spring song. Nearby another newly returned summer visitor joined in, a willow warbler, which often, like the chiffchaff and the other warblers, is heard singing long before it is seen. At last I caught sight of this one, on the top of a sycamore, where his yellow-green plumage matched perfectly the bright new leaves and unfolding flowers. The throat of this little summer visitor pulsated as his song poured forth, part territorial claim and part advertisement for a mate, but sounding to many a human ear like a thanksgiving for safe arrival and a hymn of joy for the beauty of the day. Who's to say that birdsong, over and above its mundane function, is not part of a universal celebration of life?

There was much to celebrate today, too, not only the obvious delights of birdsong and bluebells but the appearance of many other species of wild plant or creature after their long winter absence. In my garden and all around the village the lilac flowers are coming out, giving off their sweet, cloying smell which contrasts so markedly with the pungent garlic smells of two common wild flowers out now, the wild garlic and the garlic mustard. The garlic mustard, or 'Jack-by-the-hedge', is a common plant, most obvious at this time of year when its tall stems crowd thickly along the hedges, bearing heart-shaped, toothed leaves and white flowers. Though it has a smell of garlic, this plant is a member of the cabbage family, and as its name suggests was once used as a culinary herb. The wild garlic or ramsons belongs to the lily family, but grows in the shadier hedgerows and, particularly, in deciduous woods such as Eaves Wood where it often forms thick carpets of white flower-heads and rather fleshy leaves which resemble somewhat those of an aspidistra, but, even more so, the leaves of the lily of the valley, to which it is related. These leaves give off what many consider to be a rank smell. For me it is one of the characteristic scents of spring and therefore very welcome.

Even more welcome are the first orange tip butterflies which appeared this afternoon, in the lanes and gardens of the village. The males are unmistakeable, having large, orange-coloured patches on the tips of their forewings. Their restless dance-like flights are performed in search of the females, which lack the orange patches and are less conspicuous, to the human eye at any rate. These butterflies usually emerge in April, but they are seen in such numbers now because the food plants for their caterpillars are flourishing, especially the favoured garlic mustard and other plants of the crucifer family such as the cuckoo flower or lady's smock, which is currently showing itself on my lawns among the cowslips.

These lawns would never be selected to appear in those infuriating and mendacious gardening magazines which like to present us with images of the perfect lawn, flawless and weed-free, level and smooth as a billiard table with neat stripes to complete the effect. From that point of view my lawns are no doubt the least attractive in Silverdale, being uneven and full of rocky outcrops, and therefore difficult to maintain to that high degree of perfection beloved of all those gardeners who take themselves and their plots of ground seriously. Furthermore the grass in my lawns has to compete with various sorts of moss, as well as plantain, cowslip, dandelion, lady's smock and, later in the season, ox-eye daisies. My ancient and hard-worked mower does its best, as do I, and we set to work to take the roughness off a large part of the grass, leaving a good-sized patch where the thickest of the spring flowers are growing, creating a wildflower garden in the middle of one of the lawns which will last all summer until the cowslip seed is black and rattling in its brown capsules.

I worked on in the garden until dusk began to fall at about half past nine, by which time the butterflies were long gone and the birds were giving their evening calls before going to roost. A hedgehog snuffled about on the lawn, possibly drawn by the smell of the cut grass which to him would signify slugs and insects uncovered by the mowing. A couple of robins had earlier been to see what they could find. Now, one on either side of the wood, they kept up their clicking sound in the gloom. The stillness of the evening mirrored the calm of the day. A woodcock, that strange and mysterious wading bird which unlike all others of its kind favours woods in which to breed and spend much of its time, passed overhead with rapid wingbeats and croaking call, on its way from Eaves Wood down to the marshes to feed.

10 May

More butterflies in the garden. Cabbage whites, of course, but more colourful ones as well, including the orange tips that continue to perform their courtship flights. Handsomely marked butterflies such as peacock, red admiral, small tortoiseshell and brimstone join them. The brimstone butterfly hasn't the varied markings of these other species, being a uniform sulphur yellow, which is a most attractive sight all through the spring and summer, but especially welcome in March when it first appears, one of the earliest butterflies to emerge. All of these species passed through my garden today, but my wood had one of its own, the speckled wood butterfly, which is commonly found in limestone woodland. Several of them congregated in the dappled shade under the big oaks. It isn't a sun-lover, this insect, and doesn't need flowers so much as the others, preferring to feed on the honeydew produced by aphids. The rest of the butterflies, however, were eager to feed on those flowers offering themselves, such as the thick, conical blooms of the lilac bush and the pure white flower heads of the bird cherry, which just now brightens every corner of the garden and fills the air with its almond smell, mingling with the lilac and the bluebells to create a heady, composite fragrance drifting across the lawns and under the trees.

Beneath the trees sat a solitary roe deer, all on her own in the middle of a patch of bluebells. At the beginning of the month the family party remained undivided, but ten days later they have gone their separate ways and there now remains this solitary doe, heavily pregnant and waiting for the birth of her fawn in the solitude of our bit of wood. Her stillness disarmed any inquisitiveness on the part of my dogs, which pass by with scarcely

Roe deer on the limestone

so much as a look, though they know she is there. The land is burgeoning, new life appearing everywhere. Only this afternoon Hetty, one of the pheasant hens, appeared in the garden with half a dozen newly hatched chicks, tiny creatures covered in fluffy down, running about on the lawn like little striped, clockwork toys. Their hatching is at about the usual time, only three days later than the brood hatched in our wood last year.

11 May

The sudden appearance of Hetty with her six chicks gives new life and interest in the garden, and drama too. In fact there was mayhem in the pheasant world today, when Simon turned up and was promptly driven off by his sire, Cedric, who continues to object to the presence of one son, though not to the other. Sidney, in fact, was standing by when the altercation happened, but, opportunist and survivor that he is, seized the moment and mated with one of the hens while their lord and master was otherwise occupied. Cedric is quite content to tolerate one rival male, even at this critical time in the season, which would seem to negate the reason for being so watchful and assertive, as Sidney's behaviour proves. Sidney has his uses, however, for when a big, black crow came down to try and seize one of the chicks while Cedric's attention was directed elsewhere, he darted forward and resisted the determined predator, driving him away with the help of Cedric who returned from putting Simon to flight just in time. Spring fever is very strong just now.

12 May

A clear blue sky and a light breeze, a perfect morning except that the first hang glider of the season came over, one of the least welcome sounds of an English spring, for this was a contraption with a motor, with the irritating drone that these aerial motorcycles have. No doubt the view from up there is spectacular, especially as the machine is slow-moving and takes a long time to travel half a mile or so, but not for the first time I wondered why people can't enjoy the countryside without spending huge sums of money on equipment and making nuisances of themselves. The annoyance was soon over, however, and peace reigned again. Swallows filled the sky instead of the flying machine, dandelion seed drifted by on the breeze and a marsh harrier sailed on its huge wings up the valley from Leighton Moss, circled Hawes Water then glided back again.

Hetty only had five chicks this morning, so she has lost one overnight. It was a good thing I left some of the grass to grow, because it acts as cover for the pheasant chicks that spend time hiding there when danger threatens, as it did again today. The family group were insect-hunting in the grass round a tree-stump, the one which attracted a green woodpecker earlier in the year, then they moved away from the relative safety of the trees and onto the open lawn, where a passing crow saw its opportunity, flew down and tried to snatch one of the little feathered bundles. Hetty flew at the crow and successfully drove it off. The crows will cease their attentions in a few days, when the chicks become larger and more adept at concealment. They are in much more danger from nocturnal predators, such as rats, until they can fly and get up into the trees to roost.

The wind dropped, and after all the earlier excitement the afternoon was still, calm and hot, the hottest day of the year so far in our garden. Not surprisingly I found a slow worm basking at the edge of the lawn and picked it up without difficulty. If handled roughly they can shed the wriggling hinder part of the tail while they make their escape, like all lizards, but this beautiful, bronze-coloured, serpentine creature lay in my hands without movement, then slid slowly away when I set it down in the grass again.

A blackbird sang, and a blackcap also, blending its full, rich, melodic phrases with those of the bigger bird. Other birds seemed content to sit in the shade and remain silent, except for the occasional toot-toot of Cedric somewhere in the wood. Butterflies and other insects passed their entire day visiting the big lilac bush with its heavy-scented, thick purple flower heads. A middle-sized brown bumble bee lighted on the pinkish-red flower of herb robert growing out of a wall, bending the slender stem right down, almost to breaking point it seemed, though of course these plants are tougher than they look. Then he flew heavily across to a rosemary bush, where he buzzed about self-importantly among the delicate blue flowers. A young robin, brown and spotted and completely lacking the bright red breast of his parents, sat in a bush watching the world go by with an inquisitive, somewhat bemused expression. The garden is full of life: full of birds, of insects, of flowering plants and green, growing things of all sorts.

We ate out of doors, staying out until half past six, by which time cloud was coming over and the air was cooling. On the same day last year the fierce heat of the day had only just started to lessen by six and we sat until nine o'clock under boughs heavy with cherry blossom where a blackbird was singing.

13 May

Rain, and a lower temperature than yesterday's, with the swallows flying low over the lawn whereas yesterday they were high in the sky. Cedric and Sidney sat or stood in the open on the grass, doing nothing apart from getting wet. Hetty was about with her chicks but soon went under the shelter of the lilac bush with them. She still has five, which she keeps close to her with a proper matronly concern, but her new status as mother didn't stop Sidney from displaying to her and even mating with her when the opportunity arose. His father, Cedric, shows a remarkable tolerance to this opportunistic youngster, who last summer was, so to speak, the runt of his father's various litters, lowest down the pecking order and on the receiving end of much intolerance and bullying.

14 May

The rain continues. Hetty sheltered under the lilac bush all night. She ran across ten yards of lawn this morning to feed very quickly, then after only a few seconds ran back to her chicks again. She takes great care of them. They stayed in the same relatively sheltered spot all morning. Meanwhile, as we watched the pheasants, a roe deer was born in the wood, an event which takes place in this quiet spot every year. We missed the birth, but later, when we turned our attention to the trees at the back of the house, suddenly the striped kid was there, getting uncertainly to its feet then beginning to feed straight away. Later still we watched it as it tottered away on its spindly legs, following its mother across the clearing in our wood to an even more secluded place. With so much woodland round about, the fawn could have been born in any one of a number of places in the neighbourhood, but the likelihood is that our patch of trees offers more peace and quiet than many others, where there is frequent disturbance on and around any footpath or public area. Roe deer often have two fawns, more properly called kids, which they separate soon after the birth, so this one may well have a twin hidden somewhere not far away.

17 May

Hetty has only three chicks surviving this morning. They disappear, one by one, in the night, while they are hidden snugly in the thick ground cover at the edge of the wood, suggesting a ground predator such as a rat, which could easily find out where they were. Last year the same thing happened, to Hatty, the only other hen of Cedric's so far this year. She began with a brood of ten that had shrunk to seven by the next day. By the following morning the remainder had been taken, leaving poor Hatty with nothing. In the end four of Cedric's offspring survived, three to a hen we called Hilda and one to Hermione, the chick which grew to become Sidney the Survivor.

I stood in the doorway, watching the three chicks, which wandered erratically on the lawn picking at tiny insects and the smallest of slugs. Letting the grass grow here and there as cover for the pheasants allows all sorts of other things to hide of course, including the slugs, but the toads and hedgehogs eat some of the larger ones, and the small birds, with their ravenous broods of nestlings, pick up the smaller invertebrates. A healthier balance of nature is establishing itself in my garden, in which everything depends upon everything else. Daisies and buttercups are growing among the grass, along with red clover, purple vetch, the china-blue flowers of germander speedwell and, still flourishing, a host of cowslips. These in their turn act as food plants for a multitude of creatures, from the roe deer down to butterflies.

The depleted pheasant family retreated to the shelter of the lilac bush, which is still heavy with rich purple blooms. The chicks seem hardly any bigger after a week, but they are gaining in confidence and daring, after the manner of young creatures of all sorts. Following their mother, two of the three flapped their stubby wings and jumped in the air in a comical attempt at flight. Meanwhile, as I stood and watched, the blue tits kept coming to the nest box only inches away from my head, with bright green caterpillars clutched in their beaks to feed their newly-hatched young. I felt I ought to move away before I was offered a caterpillar myself.

A walk along the lanes seemed called for. Never a better time to walk along an English lane than when the hawthorn blossom is out, and now is the time, with bush after bush of it showing masses of cream coloured flowers. I am tempted to record that it is a very good year for may blossom, but looking back I don't remember a bad year, and hawthorn is one of those trees which never disappoints, though in some years, certainly, there are fewer hawthorn berries than ever. I suppose we should now go about casting clouts, unless the old rhyme refers to the month of May, not the flower, but in that case, for greater clarity (though in infinitely poorer verse) we should, in the modern revisionist spirit, chant:

> *Don't go without your pullover*
> *Until the month of May is over*

Anyway, the hawthorn bushes are glorious now, and the lanes are filled with a sort of surging white tide of flowers, including mayflowers, cow parsley, wild garlic, jack-by-the-hedge and, now and then, a massive pyramid-shaped horse chestnut covered in its large, white, conical flowers or 'candles' as children used to call them.

The leaves on the horse chestnut are also fully open, large, spread-out leaves with five or six lobes like the fingers of giant hands. In Eaves Wood and my own wood the tree canopy is thickening, the leaves of oak, wych elm, and sycamore of course, gradually filtering the light and blocking the sun from the flowers on the ground. However, not all the trees are in leaf, most notably the ash, and we are still delighting in the masses of bluebells, which have increased since I started to thin the wood and let more light in. Plants which are tolerant of shade are thriving, too, such as my wild garlic which is at last showing itself, as well as the sweet woodruff and the stitch-wort, which supports its straggling stems by clinging on to surrounding grasses or other vegetation.

25 May
Just across the lane from our garden is the quaintly named Letter Box Field where the grass is allowed to grow as a crop of hay. Since first coming to live in this quiet and unspoiled place we have marvelled each year at how, when the winter grazing is finished, the grass is left to grow, not just for an early cut of silage and one or two more later on, but as a traditional hay meadow, one in which many sorts of meadow grasses grow, grasses with familiar names which are almost as old as England itself. Names like an illuminated manuscript of English life and tradition: foxtail and fescue, cocksfoot and quaking grass, timothy, rye grass and Yorkshire fog. In amongst them are a few specimens of ranker vegetation, some plantains, docks and a handful of thistles, and some clusters of flowers which add splashes of colour to the green: the russet of sorrel and the butter-and-cream look of buttercups and cow parsley.

Elsewhere fields have already been cut for silage, which stands in black plastic skins like so many oversize black puddings on the stubble which is a sickly yellow at first before it greens up again. The whole thing seems like a miracle in this age of profit and efficiency, a crop left to mature in its own time, not ploughed up and seeded with a monoculture, but harvested in due course, leaving shelter and abundant food in the meantime for a host of small creatures, insects, voles and field mice for example, and the larger animals which feed on them in turn: owls, kestrels, buzzards, stoats – and so on. Our roe deer has taken her kid in there, knowing it can lie still all day and not be seen. The doe herself, when she lies down in it, is hidden up to the shoulder, and our pheasant cock, when he promenades across the lane for a change, has only his head visible in the long grass when he stands up straight to look around. After two or three days of rain this grass has been well-watered, and now on this sunny, bright afternoon it is receiving the light and warmth it also needs to mature, though it is already tall, and rip-pling like a lake in the breeze.

26 May

Tiny and insubstantial as the pheasant chicks still are, vulnerable and easily taken, these bundles of down are lively and always growing, learning and developing. I have been watching them feeding among the grasses, where they take a speculative peck at a seed head and help themselves deftly, with inborn skill, to some small fly or minute slug which their sharp eyes have detected. At first their mother guarded them closely, clucking to them to encourage them to move along in secret, sheltered places in the ceaseless search for food. Now she can leave them under the lilac or in the long grass and come to feed with the other pheasants when I put out seed in the morning. Now it is their turn to call to her, cheeping incessantly when they want her to come back so that she has to return before she has eaten her fill.

Sometimes the chicks venture out into the open as well, in which case Hetty can feed for a bit longer. Joining in with the communal feeding, the youngsters risk an occasional peck from their father or an aunt. Even at this tender age they are learning that life has a pecking order, literally in their case, and that for the time being they are at the bottom of it. To add insult to injury they are even trodden on by their own mother, which I have seen happen more than once. The hapless chick is flattened under the spreading toes of the hen, but always springs up again like a squashed rubber ball. The chicks can now fly properly over short distances, so they are becoming more resilient all the time and better equipped to survive in a harsh world.

27 May

A warm, sunny day with a breeze which the swallows seemed to relish, skimming the waving meadow grass as if they wanted to start the hay harvest themselves by scything the feather-like seed heads. Swifts, on the other hand, soared high over the village and swept on sickle wings in steep downward curves, rushing round the tower of Saint John's Church and shrieking as if in delight at their own skill and artistry as the most supreme masters of the air.

Down at Jenny Brown's Point the breeze was stronger, leaning its weight upon the bent and twisted forms of the thorn bushes that stubbornly survive along the Point and over Jack Scout. Sheltering under this wind-burnt scrub of blackthorn, hawthorn and dog rose were yellow clusters of flowers tinged with red, the bird's foot trefoil, known to young and old when I was a boy as 'bacon and eggs'. I had the place to myself on this breezy Monday afternoon in May, with only a roving, inquisitive family of great tits to share the solitude as I sat on a bench and looked out to sea.

The tide had turned, but the wind was whipping the waves up and holding back the sea along the sloping, rocky shore. The glittering waters of the Bay now cover at every high tide the place where years ago we used to have picnics on the short, sheep-nibbled sea-turf, which has since been washed away by the ever-changing tides and shifting currents which move the river channels about and bite away at the land itself. One day the currents will alter again, and the peaty turf will come back to the foreshore at Silverdale.

28 May

'The rain it raineth every day'. Well, not exactly, but the April showers do seem to have saved quite a lot of themselves for May this year. It was a pity that today couldn't have been like yesterday, especially for the people who began the reed planting this morning in the next stage of the marsh reclamation project in the fields between Crag Foot and Barrow Scout. Big buckets of green reeds were brought to the site and a company of helpers, all clad in waterproofs of vivid reds and yellows, began planting them along the muddy channels. It was an uncommon sight, almost un-English, these watery fields dotted with strange, hooded, stooping figures, like rice planters in paddy fields.

Fortunately it didn't rain all day, and some of the rain was light enough to allow a walk along the lanes, where the moisture had unlocked those wonderful earth-smells and the freshness of greenery. The sun came out for a time, and the sweet scent of May blossom drifted across my garden, where the heavy-headed crimson peonies struggled to remain upright.

By the evening the land was much drier and I sat out of doors listening to the birds singing and watching the swifts and swallows soaring and

The house from the wild flower lawn

circling after late insects. A cockchafer or maybug flew heavily past me, blundering into a window and falling to the ground where it lay on its back waving its legs feebly in the air like an Edwardian gentleman slightly the worse for wear, until it righted itself again at last, as they invariably do. Our blackbird continued singing until after dark and the robins later than that, nearly eleven. All else was silent as I stood in the wood with the dogs at my heels, not a sound from kennel, farm, lane or wood, except the sudden soft thudding of hooves as the roe deer scented us and made off in the dark.

June

1 June

The month probably derives its name from the Roman goddess Juno, the queen of heaven. An altogether fitting association for such a regal, bountiful month, which began today in glorious sunshine. In my garden the peonies are in full flower, full, blowsy, many petalled blooms of rich crimson and pale pink. They are joined by blue cornflowers, yellow poppies, scented stocks in pastel shades and coronets of crosswort set on bases of four short, ribbed, pointed petals. Honeysuckle of red and gold twines up a trellis on a garden wall and in the wood the wild variety clambers up the hawthorns and even, on woody, long-established stems, up mature oaks. Elsewhere blue or mauve wisteria hangs in thick clusters from its vines against cottage walls, and laburnum leans over garden walls, dripping with yellow pendant flower clusters. A cuckoo came this morning, as late as the ash leaves, to add his ironic herald's call to celebrate the richness of summer.

The ash trees are making haste now, at last, and joining the oaks, beeches, limes, sycamores, chestnuts and all the other trees, adding that full, rounded, Junoesque voluptuousness to the land. Massed together they seem the very essence of all life on the planet, for where would we be without the green leaves? What sort of a life would it be with far less tree cover than we have now, and that is precious little, except in a favoured spot like Silverdale. We rely so much on the tireless and unseen labours of the trees.

Very conspicuous labour is going on in the fields now, with the farmers and their helpers working hard to bring in the hay harvest, or its modern version, the silage crop. Everywhere people are literally making hay while the sun shines, and the grass lies in long, neat, parallel rows, dark lines on the pale grass stubble. The earliest cuts of a few weeks ago are growing rapidly again with the help of sun and rain, and are ready for a second cut, or even a third in a few cases. Tractors are out in the fields towing big grass-trailers, cages on wheels into which the fresh-cut grass is shot from a blower connected to the cutting machinery. Taking advantage of the dry weather, which is likely to end tomorrow, they worked on into the evening, taking load after load of grass into storage. The tractors and their trailers swung along the empty lanes until nearly midnight, their big headlamps blaring into the dark. In the meadow facing us the grass still stands, taller than ever.

2 June

A change in the weather again, as forecast. Rain arrived, and with it flashes of lightning, accompanied by thunder that grumbled round the hills in the afternoon. The blackbirds sang on, unperturbed as the forked lightning flickered over Castlebarrow and the thunder burst startlingly overhead. Then they fell silent, and a heavy downpour sent all the birds dashing for cover. Afterwards they sang again. Water vapour rose like smoke from the drenched but warm earth, and in the wood those wonderful smells of soil and leaf were released again by the moisture.

4 June

The light began to grow and birds to sing at four o'clock this morning. Half an hour later as I strolled across the lawn the roebuck at first stared at me incredulously, not expecting a human being to be about at this hour, then made off into the wood, barking his disapproval. This buck has been barking around the house and in the wood at dawn recently, because although the rutting season is not for another month or six weeks, it is important to emphasise his claim to the territory, especially as he has one or more does with young in it. Other bucks respond to his barking, in Eaves Wood and down near Hawes Water, an impressive and slightly eerie sound at first light in the lanes and woods as yet empty of people.

Hetty is down to only two chicks this morning from three yesterday. Perhaps she will be able to rear these two successfully to adulthood. The mortality rate among young birds is fearfully high, which is why so many species have such large broods, up to fifteen for pheasants, for example. In spite of frequent losses, the age-old impulse continues, and the woods are full of newly-fledged birds, such as the young wrens I saw being fed by one of their parents in the juniper bush near the house.

6 June

Nice to be near water in hot weather. There being an Open Day at Leighton Moss, I took my two grandchildren pond dipping there, with nets supplied by the R.S.P.B. We took up our positions on a wooden deck over the water and followed the instructions of the patient, cheerful Volunteers who undertook not only to keep an eye on us all but to put names to the insects and other invertebrates we brought up from the muddy water. It was a delight to see so many young children enjoying themselves, without the benefit of interpretation boards, interactive displays, computer games or any of the other paraphernalia deemed necessary to modern education and entertainment.

Pond dipping

It was a timeless scene, really, just a group of young children together with an assortment of adults more than willing to be children again for a brief space, dipping in the water with large nets for such highly important captures as a mayfly larva, a leech and a water louse. The years rolled back as once again I saw a stickleback in a net, then a diving beetle and a water boatman, and I remembered being taught how to tickle a caddis fly larva with a straw so that at last it wriggled out of its carefully constructed tube of sand grains or minute bits of reed. Then, following its unceremonious eviction, it could be watched in wonder in an aquarium tank or goldfish bowl as it straight away set about building itself a new home of whatever brightly-coloured fragments we provided it with.

I remembered also being puzzled why my tadpoles or sticklebacks had a habit of quickly turning into shrivelled husks whenever I put them into the same container as a leech. It was some time before I discovered why their watery home had become a watery grave. Generally I was left to make all such discoveries on my own. Fifty years ago no one thought anything of a child carting home jam jars full of tadpoles and other water beasts, but times have changed and the emphasis now is on humane investigation and subsequent return of one's captives to the element from whence they came. Quite right too!

10 June

I heard the rattle of a mistle thrush this morning and looked up to see one chasing a sparrow hawk which flew so close to the house that it nearly came in at the open window. Later I saw the thrush feeding one of its young on the lawn, so the reason for its vigilance and defiance was clear. The sparrow hawk prefers to surprise its prey in flight, rather than pounce on them on the ground, so it still seems likely to me that Hetty's chicks have been the victim of rats and stoats rather than predators from the air, but a crow or a hawk cannot be ruled out.

Our pheasant family consists at present of the cock, Cedric, his three hens Hetty, Hatty and the latest arrival, Hannah, as well as Hetty's two remaining chicks. Also the youngster from last year, Sidney the Survivor, who is with the group on most days and seems to fulfill the role of older brother and general lookout. He is certainly the tamest of them, coming to stand on the steps of the conservatory and peer through the glass at us sitting reading, as if he would like to come and join us, if he could fathom out what we were up to. It certainly isn't hunger which prompts him to do this, because he comes to peer at us when he has just finished eating, so it must be pure curiosity.

Cedric can be capricious in his tolerance of other pheasants. Invariably he drives off other cocks from his territory, but mostly he puts up with Sidney who seems both companion and, to some extent, co-defender. At the feeding place, where I still put out seeds for the pheasants, the chicks and hens alike receive a casual peck from Cedric now and then, though it has all the appearance of self-assertion and group dominance rather than outright aggression.

The chicks are growing well, having reached the size of a partridge by now. They have learned to hold their own and to roam about unsupervised, though they quickly rejoin their mother when alarmed, running quickly on their noticeably longer legs. They have taken to climbing on the rocks at the back of the house and finding their way to the side, along the top of an old, solid stone retaining wall, eight feet high and two feet thick which was constructed long ago on an outcrop of rocks and stones. There the chicks stand, high above the ground, framed by the dark leaves of ivy, the little pink flowers of shining cranesbill and the gorgeous blue flowers of creeping bellflower. They peer down into the clematis, rose and honeysuckle below them that rise up from the herb bed, then they launch themselves and fly thirty feet or so across the garden to where the adults are feeding.

I watched them do this again this morning, then when they had wandered away with the rest of their family I went out to sit in the sun and enjoy the fragrance of the herbs myself. The baby blue flowers of rosemary are still brightening this corner, and the spiky leaves of chives are embellished with purple brush-heads of flowers, but the chief delight of any herb garden is its smells. Green and purple mint leaves are growing thickly, adding their aroma to the unmistakable scent of rosemary, the two combining to evoke irresistible memories of roast lamb on Sundays. Marjoram was there, too, also sage with its furry leaves, and a small thyme plant which has somehow survived and not been swamped by the bushier herbs. These more pungent but evocative smells are joined by the sweeter scents of the yellow honeysuckle, and of my climbing rose, a variety named Handel, creamy white with pink edges. Climbing and rambling roses I love, but I must say I can never summon up any enthusiasm for bush roses, not those sorts anyway which exist as barbed sticks in a sterile bed of naked earth all their lives, just for the sake of a few showy blooms in the summer.

The only problem with so much going on, the young birds in every third bush, gorged with caterpillars yet still ravenous, the bees and butterflies eager to get to the flowers, and so on, is that you can sometimes feel like an intruder in your own garden. Having retreated into the house I stood watching wood mice scampering along the limestone rocks just a few feet away from an upstairs window, whisking in and out of the crevices as if they were playing hide and seek, but in all probability, like almost every other wild creature just now, hunting for food to give to a nestful of hungry youngsters.

As I watched them I became aware of the gradual approach of a Roe deer, the kid from last season which is now a yearling and spending much of the time on her own following the separation of the family group earlier in the spring. Sometimes she can be seen in the company of the buck, her father, but often she appears suddenly, quietly from the thicker parts of the wood, a solitary animal constantly seeking food, though only for herself for the time being. Next year she is likely to be a mother herself for the first time, but for now she has only herself to think of, and like all roes she has to eat about three or four per cent of her weight in food every day, hence her boldness now in clambering along the uneven rocks so close to the house, where she nibbled the leaves and flowers of bramble. Roe deer have highly developed hearing and sense of smell, but the ones which frequent our wood and garden are used to us and take no notice if we keep still. This one was now so close that I could see she has an infection around one of her eyes that has caused a swelling. I hope it gets no worse, for her sight is important to her despite the fact that she is a woodland dweller and relies on the other senses so much. How vulnerable all young animals are.

16 June
Two hundred years ago today Dorothy Wordsworth recorded in her journal that the swallows with their ' forked, fish-like tails' were coming close to her bedroom window, where she expected them to build their nest. Later they did so, but the nest collapsed and fell to the ground, so had to be rebuilt, which sounds as though the birds were house martins rather than swallows, but Dorothy regularly recorded the appearance and behaviour of birds, as did her brother William in his poems, an indication of her delight in nature and close observation of it. She took special pleasure in the swallows and martins, which is easy to understand, especially now when many of them already have young in the nest which they are working hard to feed with the beakfuls of insects they are constantly gathering in their low, swooping flight under trees, across fields and over water. At Leighton Moss today the

swallows were in company briefly with both sand martins and house martins, all skimming the surface of the meres, dipping occasionally to drink before resuming their quest for food.

Such a common sight, swallows dipping over a pond, yet one of those many natural wonders of which we never grow tired. This constant sweeping low over water led our ancestors to conclude that the mud at the bottom of ponds was where they hibernated when they disappeared in the autumn. In the eighteenth century the pioneering naturalist, Gilbert White, in an attempt to prove or disprove the theory, caused local ponds to be dragged near his Hampshire home. It seems to me that we need both the Wordsworthian approach to nature and that of White and his successors: the poetical and the investigative. After all they are both motivated by the same love of, and interest in, the workings of nature.

It is to be hoped that the swallows continue to return to our barns and outbuildings, for that is where they principally build their nests, though before Man the Builder arrived on the scene swallows must have been predominantly cliff and cave nesters. Recently there have been instances of swallows building their nests in a cave along the shore at Silverdale, a very rare occurrence in Britain in modern times. If they always had to rely on natural rock ledges for their nest sites however, swallows would be much less numerous than they are, but their numbers could well be diminished by a lack of available nesting space if current trends continue. Barns are being converted to dwellings at a rapid rate and people no longer leave their outhouses unlocked with the doors and windows open as used to happen, because of the greater need for security. All this to add to the natural hazards in the swallows' winter quarters in southern Africa and the drought and deserts they have to face on migration, as well as the continuing onslaught from European 'sportsmen', with their barrage of guns, their limed twigs and mist nets. Recent dramatic declines in once common and well-loved species such as the song thrush and the house sparrow show that we cannot take for granted the unassisted survival of any sort of wild plant or animal. We have to be vigilant.

Vigilance of a different kind was rewarded today, with the sighting of a bittern at Leighton Moss. I was there when a small group of excited birdwatchers trained their binoculars and telescopes on the rarity, which appeared near the edge of one of the reedbeds and stood, half hidden in the reeds which are the same colour as itself, and which are its complete world, the place where it lives, feeds, nests, roosts and survives the whole year round. Take away the reedbeds and the bittern is finished. Therein lies the problem. The bittern was once, long ago, quite common in the fens and marshes of England, but land has been drained for centuries, and the demands of agriculture, the growth of towns and other pressures caused by phenomenal population growth in humans has taken a severe toll. Even such apparently unrelated social change as the wholesale abandonment of thatched roofs in favour of tile and slate leads to the bittern's habitat no longer being needed as a resource for human life, with the resulting neglect or clearance of the reedbeds. Such a specialised bird as the bittern is easily wiped out from whole areas when radical change takes place in the landscape.

Still, the species continues to survive, thanks to the efforts of conservationists, especially the Royal Society for the Protection of Birds, at whose Reserve of Leighton Moss a few bitterns survive in secret, watery, eel-enriched bliss. Numbers fluctuate, but the current breeding population consists of only two pairs, an indication of the rarity of the bird. Hence the excitement of the birdwatchers when a bittern shows itself, for many people come to Leighton Moss year after year and never see one. They may well catch a glimpse of the other rare birds of the reserve. The marsh harrier of course is often to be seen flying round the reeds during the summer months, and even the elusive bearded tit or reedling is to be seen when the family parties take to wandering about the Reserve in late summer. But a bittern? To some birdwatchers it seems almost a legendary creature, as fabulous as a phoenix and as likely to be met with. Today's visitors to the Moss were among the lucky ones, catching sight of this secretive, heron-like bird which was well aware of their presence on the opposite side of the mere and regarded them with a long, appraising stare from the glaring yellow eyes set well forward at the front of the head, close to that efficient-looking, dagger-like beak. When nature confronts you like that, you feel drawn into it, and today couldn't have been a better day for the sighting, with the swallows flying, the reed warblers singing lustily in the gently swaying reeds and the bright flowers of yellow loosestrife and yellow iris like a sort of dusting of gold setting the seal on everything.

20 June
Sunny and very warm, the sort of day we expect in June but don't always get. I retreated into the wood where a woodpigeon soothed the heat of the day with its crooning and the hart's tongue ferns protruded from cracks in the limestone as if the earth itself were panting with exhaustion and were responsible for the specks of saliva decorating the woodland sedges. In sober truth this was the cuckoo spit I have known since boyhood, when I made the momentous discovery that it was not the product of some expectorating bird but a secretion of protective liquid, filled with air bubbles, covering a tiny insect during its development in the nymph stage. This insect was the froghopper, which endeared itself to us boys partly because the vulnerable little creature created such a cunning disguise for itself, which fooled lesser predators than ourselves. Mainly, though, we liked it because in its adult stage it would often land on us and show no fear, then leap away again with awe-inspiring agility if we so much as touched it gently with a finger tip.

These days the froghoppers have nothing to fear from prying eyes and restless, childish fingers, and they live undisturbed in their carefully constructed but frothy and insubstantial worlds. In any wood, especially one established on limestone with a diverse flora and fauna, there are any number of miniature worlds and private lives being lived out that the casual observer never sees. High up in the trees there are butterflies and other insects whose presence is hard to detect unless they come closer to the ground by accident or design. Even on the ground itself are countless secret communities of plants and insects living in the grikes or fissures in between the great slabs of rock, the limestone clints. There are different parts of the wood with distinct character, from the hog's back running up the middle with its mosses, ferns and dog's mercury, to the eastern edge where the hazel has been coppiced to encourage flowers to grow and butterflies to breed. All this within an acre and a half, 'so much variety in so small a space' as the nature writer Wynford Vaughan-Thomas once said about the British Isles as a whole.

23 June

A time of radiant, golden dawns, and of skies of rose-pink, dove-grey and acquamarine at dusk, 'the earth filled with swelling ecstacy' as Henry Williamson put it in one of his essays. That ecstatic state is illuminated by the strange brilliance on the land, a special light shining on woods, fields and gardens, morning noon and night, to emphasise the abundance and diversity of life there. All living things have a consciousness of their own being which is quickened by the warmth of the sun, the sweetness of the air, the pulse of the earth and the proximity of other life around them.

The birds are busy from before daylight until after dusk feeding their nestlings, in some cases second broods, or downy, gormless fledglings just left the nest and ranged along the branches, offering yellow gapes for food at any adult bird that passes. The insects are as busy as ever with their reproductive cycle, too, and even the mammals have their work cut out to keep their growing young well-fed, in their case because their prey doesn't lie down and offer itself to be eaten, but has to be pursued energetically, quite often without success. That is why the stoat, which sometimes I see crossing the lane like grease lightning, a worm-like, undulating brown thing dashing between one grass verge and another, will accept without demur the free gift of a rabbit killed by a passing car, and allow itself be seen in a motionless state for once as it tackles the carcase which is much bigger than itself, standing with one paw on it like an intrepid huntsman with one foot on the rhinoceros he has just shot.

28 June

Brilliant sun again, burning down on a lush landscape, throwing into almost surreal relief the long stems and long, blade-like leaves of a butterfly bush against the glaring white of a gable end. The orange, globe-shaped flowers hung like so many tiny replicas of the sun itself. An afternoon of brilliant colour: the orange flowers, the vivid green of grass, the indescribable, exhalted blue of the sky and the stunning white of the towering cumulous cloud. A buzzard circled higher and higher in the afternoon heat as if aiming to reach the vast plains and mountain ranges of undiscovered cloudland. From on high he looks down on a rich land, flowing with milk and honey, or, more importantly from his point of view, teeming with voles and young rabbits.

Apart from the circling hawk, nothing moved except for the bees in the mauve flowers of mallow in my garden. The birds perched in the shade of the trees and bushes. A roe deer had been through the garden in the early morning but now lay, couched and ruminating, in one of the darker recesses of the wood. Even the slow worms were immobile, though they love this weather to lie out in, on grassy banks or piles of clippings. There was not a breath of air, not even enough to shake the dangling gorgon locks of nettle flowers that move in the slightest breeze.

There was movement enough going on, slow and imperceptible, for while the animal kingdom slept in the sun, the plants continued their stealthy expansion, their growth upwards and outwards. The climbing plants are perhaps the most noticeable in this respect, for example the blue and yellow vetches scrambling up the long grass, and the goosegrass, also known as 'cleavers' because of its remarkable tenacity in cleaving or clinging to whatever it touches, reaching up from the grass which it has already conquered up into the lower sprays of hawthorn. Bryony trails along the fence rails and in the hedges, bearing large, glossy, arrowhead leaves and inconspicuous flowers. It is a common plant, but quietly successful until the autumn when it brings forth clusters of large, shiny, scarlet berries. Both berries and roots of this plant are poisonous, though they were used in healing by the old herbalists who were presumably careful about the quantities they measured out to cure their patients.

The most noticeable wildflower at the minute is the foxglove, which is also poisonous, but which was also used in medicine, like so many other plants. Tall, stately and bearing those large, purple, tubular flowers, it is a plant long associated with mystery, magic and fairy lore, as its name suggests, and its other country names of which there are many, such as 'goblin's thimbles' and 'elf gloves'. Its medicinal properties are real enough, the drug digitalis being extracted from it for use in the treatment of disorders of the heart. Growing nearby are the beetroot-coloured flowers of the hedge woundwort, which as its name suggests was also used in herbal medicine, in which it was valued as an ingredient of poultices, probably because of its antiseptic properties.

There are so many plants which were once used in practical folk medicine, and which could be again. It is certainly gross folly to dismiss as vulgar weeds those insignificant plants of the hedgerow that one-day may give up their secrets and yield the latest miracle cure. It is criminal negligence to permit so much of our countryside to disappear under concrete and for whole plant communities to be lost to science. Whether useful as culinary and medicinal herbs or not, all plants are beneficial to us and to the rest of life on the earth. Even the ugliest or the most toxic make their contribution. All plants, from the towering oak tree to the chickweed which is trodden underfoot, literally breath life into us, and without our forests, without the immense volume and variety of plant life, the world as we know it would be unable to support us any longer.

29 June

The two pheasant chicks have grown a lot in the last week. They are now bigger than full-grown partridges, and spending more time at a distance from their mother. On the gravel in front of the house this morning they were joined by a young rabbit that appeared out of nowhere. He was nearly full grown, though obviously from a relatively recent litter and still exhibiting that juvenile curiosity that all young animals have. Then a grey squirrel appeared, also a youngster. They come into our wood from time to time, when driven by the pressure of numbers elsewhere, but they never stay long, and are actively discouraged in our garden, particularly by my bull terrier, which has chased and caught quite a few of them.

The rabbit seemed rather lonely, having strayed about half a mile from his own kind. He found a temporary hiding place under the magnolia bush and behind a musk mallow, then, bored with that, he hopped up to the young pheasants, which got out of its way. It pursued the squirrel instead, but that, too, rejected his advances and made off down the drive and into the lane. His attempts to make friends coming to nothing, he too went away.

Waterslack Lane

July

1 July

We are moving towards high summer, yet today we have low temperatures, grey skies and, worse still, a wind getting up and lashing rain across the lawn, half-obscuring the still uncut hay meadow across the lane. It was early evening before the rain stopped and there were blue skies again, full of drifting clouds of grey, white, gold and pink. The grass in the meadow was still wet, but drying rapidly, and the roe doe and her kid were grazing contentedly among the tall grasses, watching attentively when anyone passed by, without showing any signs of wanting to move.

3 July

A radiantly sunny day. A young thrush hopping about in the garden. Crow, jay and magpie families visiting, and a family of goldfinches fluttering among seeding grasses and garden weeds. Young birds everywhere.

The burgeoning of summer flowers continues, with new ones showing themselves daily. My sage bush is in flower and, less welcome, the white flowers of ground elder, a plant which horrifies most gardeners because it is tenacious, spreads vigorously and covers the ground very efficiently, precisely the reasons in fact why gardeners are willing to pay good money for certain other plants from the nurseries. On the lawn selfheal is putting out its densely packed, purple flower heads among the short grass. Selfheal belongs to the mint family, though as far as I know it has never been used in cooking, like its valuable cousin, but it is another plant whose name gives a clue to its significance in times when the lowliest of plants was considered for its possible value to man. It was thought to help in the healing of wounds and throat infections.

Feverfew is another healing plant, common on walls and disturbed ground, and also found frequently in gardens, where it is just now beginning to put out its daisy-like flowers. Its name indicates that it was once believed to be capable of banishing fevers, and it is still firmly believed in by some who chew its bitter-tasting leaves as a remedy for headaches and migraines. Yet it is still treated as an undesirable weed by many who ought to know better, and rooted out, as is another member of the daisy family, the tansy, a tall, attractive plant with feathery, strongly aromatic leaves and flat-topped clusters of small, hard, disc-shaped, bright yellow flower-heads like shiny gold buttons. Tansy leaves were used as a strong flavouring in a number of dishes, including omelettes, as an alternative to expensive imported spices. In the symbolism of plants, tansy represents immortality, and though it flourishes from July to September its dried leaves were used at Easter, in the making of the popular tansy cake. In the unrelenting war being currently waged against the invasive Oxford ragwort, it is likely that some flowers which have a superficial resemblance to it will be grubbed up as well. The tansy could be one of these.

The daisy family is numerous and diverse, including ragwort, colt's-foot, yarrow, hemp agrimony and knapweed. Also such unlikely members as thistles and the dandelion and its close relatives, including cat's ear, nipplewort and hawkweed. Many of these are flowering now, and most prominent of them at the moment is the orange hawkweed, which grows well in my garden, particularly on the lawn, but I mow round it where I can because it is quite a decorative weed, with its flowers of burnt orange or brick red clustered close together, open and in bud, on the tops of slim, leafless stalks. These foxy-coloured flower clusters give the plant one of its other names, 'fox-and-cubs'.

4 July

St. John's Wort, one of the hypericum family, is growing round the edges of the wood, a flower long associated with mid-summer, with the sun and light, and therefore used as a charm to banish the forces of darkness. Its curative properties were well-known throughout Europe, and it is still widely used in herbal medicine. Nearby, a tall plant called the figwort, bearing small, two-lipped, purplish flowers, growing in the shade of an oak tree. Figwort long ago was used in the treatment of scrofula, and in poultices placed on sores, abscesses and even gangrene.

5 July

We walked to Middlebarrow Quarry, a vast empty space, now so silent and deserted after all the decades of activity and noise: the drilling and the clanking of machinery, the regular explosions, the cataclysmic falls of rock and the subsequent carrying away of boulders in heavy lorries. It is good not to have to listen to their jolting, shuddering and rumbling past our front gate all day long from six o'clock in the morning on their way through Warton and Carnforth to the motorway. No more booming explosions, either, with tremors felt in the earth from the fractured rock a mile away.

Middlebarrow Quarry

Silence reigns in the quarry now. After a while a noise might be heard, but it is only the solitary croaking of a crow in the midst of the desolate void. His kind has come suddenly into possession of a range of niches and ledges in the rock, and his voice is a sort of commentary on the silence rather than a breaking of it. Likewise the falling of a loose stone, catching as it drops a jutting rock here and there and landing on the quarry bottom far below with a crack which seems swallowed up in the emptiness. It is as if the immense layers of rock are exuding the silence of the hundreds of millions of years in which they have lain hidden. It is a humbling experience, standing before this immense cliff, measuring with the eye the tremendous thickness of some of the rock strata and trying to comprehend the almost unimaginable passage of time they represent.

All movable boulders and marketable rocks have been carried away, the remaining rubble buried and the ground smoothed over into rounded hillocks that lead down into the flat bottom. Not all of this ground is barren. A few scrubby specimens of birch and willow have been left. Coltsfoot is well established, always one of the first plants to emerge from what seems dead ground. It was possible, standing there, to envisage some future time when soil covers the rock and rubble, when trees and flowers grow there and insect life and birds temper the profound silence with their collective murmur. As a sort of token of this I found a shield bug poised on a cluster of lady's mantle, but the project lies at some time in the future, though much less than the blink of an eyelid compared to the geological immensity of time revealed in all this vastness. It is possible to imagine this whole quarry bottom softened in a short space, though the severity of the sheer, forbidding rock face will never be altered.

10 July

A stray hen came over the wall this morning from the sheep field next door. Cedric the pheasant kept his eye on her. He isn't used to birds as big as himself, especially ones that walk about in such an unconcerned manner on his patch of ground. However he decided she wasn't really a threat and left her alone. They don't come over very often, and either they find their own way back after a while, or I catch them and put them back where they belong, as I did in the spring with a young lamb which had got itself into a pickle by scrambling on to the wall and falling between it and the inner fence of wire netting. It's hard to find a little black lamb in a confined space in the pitch dark, but I managed it. People in the country look out for one another, just as the herdsmen did this morning when they drove their cattle down the lane, shutting my front gates so that the more wayward cows wouldn't lead the others astray by wandering into my garden.

I put the hen back into the field where she rejoined the others. 'Free range' hens they call them, these days, to distinguish them from those fowl denied the opportunity to walk about and scratch for food in the proper way. We invent handy names for things, which have always given Man the illusion that he is in control of nature. In that way modern science has often been like old-time magic, in which possessing the name of a thing was believed to give you power over it. I do like to see hens in a field, in the same way that I like to see cattle being driven on foot down a lane and not in trucks. Farm animals ought to be allowed to exercise their limbs, just as humans need to in order to stay healthy.

Later in the day I saw very healthy exercise going on in the rocky sheep field on Red Bridge Corner, where a man was scything thistles in the traditional manner. It could have been a scene from a medieval illustration or a woodcut by Bewick. I've used a scythe myself often enough when the grass has got too long for the mower, or the nettles and thistles need some attention, but today I contented myself with using the motor mower to trim those areas of lawn which haven't turned into a flower meadow.

As luck would have it I drove over a half-grown frog, which however hopped away unscathed because I had set the whirling blades on a high cut and they passed right over him as he crouched in the grass. I disturbed plenty of insects as well, judging by the interest the birds took in what I was doing. Blackbirds, pheasants and magpies all came to have a look, but only the robin came close up to me as I tipped the loads of grass clippings under some bushes in the wood. So close in fact that he almost got under the wheels. They are so fearless and companionable, robins, yet it isn't the same in Europe, where they avoid humans, which they clearly regard as dangerous animals. The relationship, it would seem, is only special in Britain, built up over many generations.

In another field not far away grass was being cut, baled, wrapped and carted off. The tractor was being followed there not by small birds but by black-headed gulls. Higher up there were martins, swallows and swifts after those insects which were escaping higher into the sky, like Icarus in great danger of having their wings clipped the higher they went towards the sun.

Though we learned later that the weather had been poor elsewhere in the country, we enjoyed our usual difference round Morecambe Bay, with a hot day and a luminous evening. At ten o'clock this evening the sky was still a bright cobalt blue, with dusk finally falling at eleven.

15 July

Sunny but humid. We went down on the marshes to see how summer life is faring there. We found rosebay willow herb flowering alongside the railway tracks. It was once not so common as it is now, and before the twentieth century people were content to grow it as a garden flower, but it began to spread, especially along railway embankments, so it is no surprise to find it growing here. Its other name is 'fireweed', a reference not just to its pinkish-red flowers but to its habit of springing up in ground which has been disturbed, burnt, or covered with slag heaps and other industrial waste. It proliferated after the Second World War in the many bomb-sites left in London and the other great cities.

Its cousin, the great willow herb, loves moister places, and there it was at the other side of the path in the boggier ground, surrounded by spear thistle, reeds, hogweed and other plants. Among the rushes grew the plant with dense, reddish-white flower spikes called redshank, a fitting name for something growing close to the lagoon where the wading birds of the same name were making their plaintive piping as they waded in the shallows.

This rich mixture of plant life supports a diversity of insects and other invertebrates. These included the delicate and attractive little striped field snail, bright orange soldier beetles which love to congregate on the large white umbels of hogweed, and the caterpillars of the peacock butterfly, which saw no reason why they should not use the path trod by humans to get about, because it made progress easier and quicker for them, though we had to tread very carefully in order to avoid squashing any.

We could hear the black-headed gulls before we saw them. They have colonised this part of the sea-marsh very effectively. Their noise is a constant, harsh accompaniment to a busy scene. Their chicks are well-grown, graceless adolescents in outlandish garb. Perhaps the gulls have been all the more successful this year because of the failure of the peregrine nest on the Crag behind us. Had the falcons not fallen prey themselves to wind and rain early on, they would surely have been helping themselves to a regular supply of gulls as food for their growing young.

The avocets also lost their eggs in the storms, but they began again and succeeded the second time. Several chicks were reared in two nests, and they are almost fully grown now, a wonderful sight, already looking rather elegant with their long legs, slender, upcurved bills and pied plumage. They are the centre of attention in this marvellous wetland at the edge of the marsh which stretches from Cotestones to Jenny Brown's Point. There are the gulls to watch, and they always provide lots of movement and interest, there are several sorts of duck, there are other waders such as lapwing, redshank and the two dozen black-tailed godwits which were wading in the pool today, but the avocets are unmistakable, and fascinating to watch as well, because of their rarity, grace and beauty.

Later on I watched young birds of a homelier sort in my garden: newly fledged magpies, robins and hedge sparrows, for example. There were song thrushes on the lawn discovering the art of worm-finding; there were young blackbirds skulking in shrubberies and learning how to throw leaves about and startle people. Hetty the pheasant has managed to rear her two remaining young, which are no longer really chicks but have reached the pullet stage. One is larger than the other, reddening up markedly so that we know it is a cock bird. When I put out food for them Hatty, the other of Cedric's two main hens, flies in from the hayfield, Letter Box Field as it is usually known, where she has been spending a lot of time lately. Or she runs pell-mell up our drive, looking famished and dishevelled. She feeds eagerly, then turns and runs back down the drive again, crossing the lane (though without looking both ways) and into the field. From this behaviour we conclude she has a nest somewhere, and wish her well, though I have fears for her safety, as today the tall grass in the meadow, having offered shelter for many weeks, was laid low in a single afternoon. Later pheasants were patrolling the neat, straight rows, picking up uncovered delicacies, and crows, daws, gulls and smaller birds were all following suit. No sign of any pheasant chicks. No sign, either, of the roe deer and her kid.

Among the birds profiting from the aftermath included the little male kestrel that often works the field and regularly perches on a convenient wire, or on a pole, surveying the hunting ground without having to expend energy in hovering. He seemed keener than ever to pounce on refugee voles and displaced field mice, so no doubt he has a nest full of young kestrels somewhere. He stayed at his post, literally, all evening, then his place was taken by tawny owls which hooted round the lanes. Slugs crept out of their hiding places to feed on the bruised vegetation, and toads came out to prey on the slugs. It was good hunting for all, made easier by a quarter moon, which gave enough light for text of an ordinary size to be read out of doors at eleven o'clock.

18 July
The holiday season is in full swing. There are hikers in the lanes and processions of caravans coming through the village. Rock climbers are up on the rock face at Trowbarrow late into the evening. We can see them from our garden, but decided today to go up and take a closer look. We walked along

the lane, over a stone stile then down a steep field where I recognised our young pheasant, Sidney, doing a bit of courting some distance from home. Perhaps his father has had a word with him. Crossing the railway line we came to the start of the quarry path and the remains of the old works where lime used to be burned on an industrial scale for the production of fertiliser, cement and an improved form of tarmacadam. The ruin of the works remains, one more subdued testimony to Silverdale's industrial past.

The old railway track which used to run down the hill from the quarry, bringing rock to the works, has long since disappeared, leaving only a footpath which to the untrained eye, has nothing of the industial about it. Long gone is the white dust on the trees, the thunder of quarry blasting above, the rumble of trucks coming down the incline, the clanking of the coupling, the noise of shunting trains on the Furness line hard by. It was a busy place, with up to thirty men working there, drilling the rock face by hand, then packing the drilled holes with gunpowder and hiding from the blast behind a huge single boulder which still stands in the middle of the quarry floor.

Working ceased there more than forty years ago, so that nature has had time, with a little human help, to cover some of the nakedness of the rock and provide diverse habitats for a variety of plants and animals. At Trowbarrow it is possible to form some idea of the changes that may take place at the much larger Middlebarrow Quarry in the years to come.

The digging and blasting in the hill at Trowbarrow lasted for only a hundred years, almost nothing in geological time. The hill itself had been formed by the ice sheet many thousands of years ago, from rocks laid down more than 300 million years before that. It is always an awesome thing to stand in front of a cliff, man-made or natural, and look at the solid rock which was once a liquid, and at the fossil remains of once living things preserved there as testimony of themselves and the far distant times they lived in. There are many wonderful things to be discovered less than a mile from where we live, but none more remarkable than this, the irrefutable but still astounding fact of the seemingly timeless and immovable rock having been laid down over hundreds of millions of years, in this case just from the skeletons of countless tiny sea creatures. A cubic foot of limestone is a graveyard of numberless dead.

More remarkable still, if possible, is the presence of fossil corals in the rock, proof that our cool northern lands once rested in the shallow waters of a tropical sea somewhere near the equator. Astonishing that this grey stone, the very bones of the land we live on, has crept northwards across the face of the earth during a period of time difficult for most of us to comprehend, we, the insubstantial beings who come to crane our necks at the silent strata or swarm up the cracks in gaudy costumes like so many overgrown insects coming out of the rock.

The holiday mood may be setting in, but work on the land has to go on just the same. The grass in Letter Box Field has been turned over in the last two days, and the hay harvest took place this evening, an operation that took two hours to complete, from seven until nine. A tractor pulled a baler, which followed the long lines of drying grass, scooping it up and ejecting the rectangular bales of hay out of a gate at the back to lie flat, or propped against one another on the smooth field like standing stones that have toppled with age. About half the bales were taken away and the rest were left on a trailer, covered with a tarpaulin, under the trees: a task for tomorrow.

25 July

Jam-making all morning, the wonderful smells of currant and strawberry wafting round the house. Then the inevitable washing up, but even that has its rewards. Standing at the sink, looking out of the kitchen window, I watched Hetty and her two young come to feed, joined by a magpie and two woodpigeons, all co-existing happily. Then, suddenly, the peaceful scene was shattered. Hetty and her chicks ran off as fast as they could to the shelter of the bushes, the magpie disappeared and the woodpigeons clattered off into the trees. From somewhere the magpie raised the alarm, and out of the blue three crows appeared, cawing urgently and hovering over the trees along the drive.

Guessing the likely cause of the commotion, I hurriedly dried my hands and went out to see if I was right. The crows, normally quick to leave when I am about, remained hurling abuse at the unseen enemy. Unseen by me, that is, until stepping round a bush which was hiding the drama from view, I saw that my suspicions had been correct. A big brown hawk flew reluctantly up from the lawn's edge and into the trees, leaving behind its prey, a collared dove, sprawled on the grass.

I went up to the victim, which I could see was still alive. Its eyes were open and it shuddered as it crouched with its wings spread. There was a raw patch on the back where the sparrow hawk had already begun to pluck out the feathers with her curved beak, holding down the prey with her sharp talons. Many of these loose feathers were scattered around on the grass. There might be a chance to save the dove, I thought, and I was reluctant to leave it where it was because the hawk might return. I stooped to pick it up, but as soon as I touched it, up it sprang having revived enough to want to avoid what it saw as more danger. It leapt into the air and flew away rapidly across the lawn, to freedom as I fondly hoped, but that instant the sparrow hawk left the trees, where she had been on the watch, and flew off in hot pursuit. The two birds sped across the lane, over the hayfield and the railway line and out of sight, the hawk eager for her dinner, the dove fleeing for its life. I don't suppose the dove survived unless it found a convenient bush to dive into, but after all collared doves are common enough, and sparrow hawks must live.

We discovered another casualty later on. In the lane lay the body of a pheasant, which we recognised as Hatty, the most senior of Cedric's wives.

She hadn't been run over but had been the victim of the trimming of the grass verges. The Council vehicle had passed inexorably her way this afternoon, and she had sat tight on her nest as the flail or cutter bars passed right over her. Then she must have panicked. If she had continued to sit still, she would have been unharmed. As it was, she lay dead beside her nest, her neck broken. Ten round, perfect eggs of a uniform, soft olive brown lay in the hollow in the grass, ironically undamaged by the passage of the machine and still hidden from view.

26 July
After a succession of dull, sometimes wet days, today was sunny and warm, so we walked through Eaves Wood and up to Castlebarrow. Several cars were parked at the beginning of the footpath, but we saw not a living soul during our walk. The wood was warm and full of dappled sunlight, wrapped in the languid stillness of high summer and silent except for the piping of an inquisitive warbler now and then. Only a teeming ant hill showed the continuing vigour of communal and reproductive life. The worker ants toiled through the undergrowth, across the footpath and up the crowded slopes bearing leaf fragments and other morsels for the sustenance of the colony or the extension of its boundaries. One of them was carrying a tiny, blue-barred jay's feather like a banner up the ramparts.

There is plenty to occupy the ant-millions in their ceaseless forestry. There are fallen trees which have not been dragged away or cut up but left to decay naturally and provide shelter and food for huge numbers of invertebrates and the small mammals and birds which feed on them. There is of course an abundance of leaf litter, too. Beech leaves seem to last the longest, except for pine needles. Sycamore seeds are also resistant to decay. Some of those from last autumn are still there, joined now by some unripe ones from this season, still green and fallen prematurely.

There are still shade-loving flowers to be seen in the wood, from the giant bellflower, showy and pale blue in the shadows, to the quaintly named enchanter's nightshade, an unobtrusive member of the willow herb family with small white flowers. It once had a big reputation, as long ago as Anglo-Saxon times, as a charm against spells cast by wood demons. Still the trees themselves, as always, claim most of the attention. Now in their full summer glory, there are mature oaks and birches, sycamores adding considerably to the shade, their bark covered with a yellow lichen, a huge beech bearing a bracket fungus big enough to sit a small child on, and pine trees scenting the air with the fragrance of their gum.

We came out at last into the open on top of Castlebarrow, two hundred and fifty feet above sea level, where the larger trees fall away and are replaced by stunted sloe and hazel bushes, and tiny ash trees grow with determination out of the clefts in the rock. The flowering plants were those of the open limestone: yellow rock rose, wild thyme and wood sage. The eye is soon lifted from the plants underfoot to the famous 'Pepper Pot' as it is known locally, the monument put up to mark Queen Victoria's Golden Jubilee in 1887. A drum or cylinder crudely fashioned from available rock fragments and wearing a conical cap, it has the appearance, to some at least, of a peppershaker. It is certainly a local landmark, a useful rallying point for walkers who get separated in the woods, and a convenient place to stand or sit and admire the view.

What a view it is too, or rather a series of views. Just below the hill lies the sprawling village, its full extent hidden away among the trees. From above Silverdale looks like a village in a wood, rather than one merely surrounded by trees. At its heart stands the red-roofed church, the stone tower rising like a beacon above the houses. Gardens merge with woods and green fields which run down to the shore, where long ago there was so much activity to do with fishing, the shipping of cattle, crossing the sands by carriage or on foot, and the transportation of the products from local industries such as quarrying and copper smelting.

The Bay must once have been dotted with small vessels, even some larger ones, but there was scarcely one to be seen today, though the tide was in, quite a high one of about twenty-seven feet. The glittering, silver-blue waters were sufficient attraction in themselves, together with distant prospects of Lancaster, Morecambe and Heysham in the haze.

28 July

The fullness of summer already contains within it the fruitfulness of autumn. I have seen the first ripe blackberries even though brambles everywhere are in full bloom. The last elder flowers are over and the green berries forming. The rose hips are still green too, but fully formed, as are the hazelnuts. Interesting how those fruits which come most readily to the eye are those which are edible or of use in wine-making.

In my garden the flowers of the moment include bellflowers, two kinds, the creeping and the clustered, as well as the hawkweeds, betony, and scabious, which is a member of the teazel family with attractive flat flower heads of powder blue, each composed of individual florets. It was also once called the 'ladies' pin cushion', and was used as a cure for skin ailments. Also vigorously flowering is the hemp agrimony, a shrub-like plant five feet tall with hemp-like leaves and quantities of dense, pinkish-red flower heads. According to the old-time herbalists it was a rough and ready purgative and, like many other plants, yielded juice that helped in healing wounds. Like the alkanet, though much taller, the hemp agrimony stands on either side of my gate, bidding welcome and farewell to visitors. The alkanet, that flower of the early spring, earlier than the bluebells, is still in bloom even now, whereas the bluebells themselves are now dry, brittle stalks which leave the soil at a touch. The sweet-smelling blue flowers are now no more than cup-shaped, paper-thin seed husks with loose black seed in the bottom.

29 July

The breeding season for the birds is past its height, though the garden is still full of young birds, which in the summer heat are competing for a space at the shallow stone trough we keep as a bird bath. Many people remember to put out food for the birds in winter, but water for them in the summer is just as important. At one point a pheasant chick and a woodpigeon were in the bath at the same time, but places in the water can be hotly contested. A robin came to bathe, then a hedge sparrow, and there was harmony between the species, but a young robin came to challenge its parent and a fight ensued. There was also rivalry between a cock and a hen blackbird for possession of the bath, but alternatives to water bathing were available, and I witnessed several birds dust bathing, and some of them indulging in that curious practice known as 'anting'. I watched a pair of jays in a 'spread eagle' or 'phoenix' posture, straddling the entrances to ant colonies, placing ants beneath their feathers, perhaps because the formic acid ejected by the ants, defensively but in vain in such instances, stimulates the skin and helps keep parasites in check. A hen blackbird also went in for the same thing, becoming so ecstatic in the process, as birds often do when anting, that she staggered about afterwards before finishing off her self-cleansing by flying to the trough and immersing herself in the water.

It was a languid afternoon, hot and humid, so like the birds we felt ourselves drawn to water and went for a walk round Hawes Water, where plumed reeds stood taller than a man, and thick, extensive stands of meadow sweet flourished alongside hemp agrimony, creamy white and pink-purple, like the mixture of colours in a dish of blackberries and cream. Along the edges of the narrow footpath, at a much lower level, crept the silverweed, an often-overlooked plant with flowers like those of buttercups and leaves with silver-coloured undersides.

Down at Leighton Moss the colour of the moment seems to be purple, with the reeds in flower together with purple loosestrife and great willow herb. Patrician colours for a time of ease. The gulls are all gone, and the geese are away at the marshes, leaving the water free for the sooty young of coot and moorhen. The ducks are in their eclipse plumage, that moulting state when the sexes resemble one another and their dabbling seems less purposeful than it usually does. A marsh harrier sat still on a tree stump. All the birds were inactive, as if waiting for rain, and the tall, grey figure of a heron at the edge of a reedbed looked like any human angler, in that he seemed hardly to care if he caught anything or not but was just waiting there for form's sake. A still, calm scene, but very warm, even at the waterside.

August

1 August

Cloudy but brightening after rain as the new day came into being. The light only starts to grow at about four in the morning now, but the shortening of the days is not obtrusive yet. In my wood the stillness was not broken but enhanced by the lilting laugh of a green woodpecker, the soft chucklings and affectionate murmurings of the crow family in the safety of the trees, and the short song of a wren, short but unmistakable as if he is singing 'everybody knows who I am, so I don't need to waste my breath.'

I went down to the Causeway at Leighton Moss, which was deserted at seven o'clock this morning except for a group of promenading pheasants, to which an immature moorhen had attached itself as a small child will hang on to a group of older boys and girls. Surrounded by reeds, I stood still and waited to see what might happen. Before long I heard a 'too-ee' call nearby and gave an imitative whistle myself in return. It wasn't long before an inquisitive willow warbler came to see what I was up to. Then it uttered its song also, rare in August when the birds nearly all fall silent.

Encouraged by my success I tried the sucking noise on the back of my hand to see what else could be attracted, and a group of reed warblers arrived to see what manner of creature I was. They were all around me, calling to one another in the reeds as they searched for insect food. I marvelled at their disregard for my presence, though I knew they would disappear quickly enough if I so much as moved a muscle. When they finally moved

Leighton Moss and Warton Crag

deeper into the reeds their place was taken by a sedge warbler, distinguishable from the reed warblers by its prominent eye stripe and streaked back. Both species are not so much secretive as living in an environment where they are not easily seen, showing themselves rarely and generally keeping down below the reed tops to avoid being seen and taken by predators, so it is always a treat to see them like this at close quarters.

Like the birds, the insects were out and about in some numbers, though not so welcome because they were mostly flies and gnats which showed a determination to get to know me as well as they could. Luckily I had remembered to dab on some insect repellent that kept them at a reasonably comfortable distance. I slid thankfully out of their reach into the shelter of the Public Hide and sat on a wooden bench to look out over the silver-grey water that was tinged suddenly with gold as the sun came through the cloud. Common reed and bulrushes fringed the mere, together with the yellow flag or iris, whose flowers have now turned into long, three-sided pods of a triangular cross section, splitting in a toothy grin to reveal rows of seeds like those on a corn cob.

Silence reigned, except for a coot making a sound like the grating of a rusty gate, to encourage its squeaking young to leave the shelter of the marginal vegetation. The coot chicks sport a piebald, downy plumage that looks shaggy and unkempt, like that of old clothes kept to wear in the garden. Leaving the hide I stepped out onto the Causeway again, just in time to see a water rail as it crossed the broad path from one reedbed to another, a bird like a moorhen in general shape but brown-backed, slate grey underneath and with striped flanks. That's usually the best sighting one can hope to have of one of these elusive birds, though I have seen them out on the grass at the gamekeeper's cottage not far away, feeding alongside moorhens, collared doves and all sorts of commoner birds.

At the end of the Causeway I turned into the footpath heading along the edge of the Reserve in the direction of the Lower Hide. I remembered the days thirty years ago when, as a conservation volunteer, I helped to make this path, at a time when the existing grass paths were being worn away by the steady increase in visitors. With a wheelbarrow and a shovel I brought one load after another of coarse gravel and other rock fragments from a heap deposited at the end of the Causeway after being brought from Trowbarrow Quarry. The number of visitors has increased many times since then, and the path has taken a lot of pounding, but, it seemed to me as I walked along it this fine summer morning, it was in its humble, utilitarian way a symbol of all that is good about the conservation of wildlife in Great Britain. Great masses of people are being made aware not only of the beauty of our countryside but its fragility, too, yet at the same time they are being encouraged to visit that countryside and see its glories at close quarters, though always with respect and restraint.

The Lower Hide offered a different view of the big mere, one in which the sunlight seemed to dance as it glinted on the shimmering water, that had alighted on a reed stem, I nearly missed the progress of another group of brownish, long-tailed reed-birds passing across the Causeway from one mass of reeds to the next. Another species which spends its life hidden in the reeds and is therefore seldom seen, the bearded tit, or 'reedling' as it is also called, is another rare species, both locally and nationally, with only sixty-five pairs at Leighton Moss and about five hundred pairs in the entire country. They were gone so quickly that I hadn't time to count them properly, but I certainly saw three of them, and I knew I had caught part of a group, probably a family party. The last of them was an adult male, which perched obligingly for me on the outermost reed stems before disappearing after the others into the protection of the thickest growth. He was a handsome bird, with back feathers of a tawny colour, a slate-blue head and the distinctive, black, moustache-like markings on the face from which the species gets its name. Though their numbers are small, bearded tits thrive pretty well if left to their own devices, so long as there are reedbeds of sufficient extent for them to live in. The conserving of existing reedbeds and, where possible, their extension or establishment on watery ground, is vital to the continued survival of this charming but elusive bird.

3 August

A day and a half of rain, from which emerged bedraggled magpies, pheasants and woodpigeons. The smaller birds seem to have been able to shelter more effectively, but by this afternoon were very hungry, having endured a period of fasting to avoid bedragglement. As well as the usual garden birds on the lawns and in the bushes, a pair of swallows fed seven fledglings as they sat on the telephone wires close to the house.

4 August

At Leighton Moss again. Little to see from the hides: herons, coot, moorhens, drab ducks, a reed warbler showing itself now and then. The gulls now completely gone and the geese still absent. Just as the holiday makers come to Silverdale for a bit of summer bird watching, the water birds are dispersing and the perching birds on the Moss are hidden in the reeds feeding their young, but there is always something to be seen, and patience is often rewarded in some way or other.

I was on the Reserve early, so there were few birdwatchers, either. There were moth-watchers, however. A group of lepidopterists had gathered, mostly male and for the most part tall, burly individuals, in pursuit of elusive, fragile creatures of the night. Like many of the moths they had caught in their overnight traps, they were all dressed drably, sporting those sleeveless, many-pocketed jackets, which are the preferred garb of their sub-species, the British Naturalist. At half-past eight this morning they gathered for the inspection of the moth traps set the previous evening, for the recording of their captures and for the subsequent enjoyment of a full English breakfast as the culmination of the event at Myers Farm the RSPB Headquarters. It would be unkind as well as untrue to say that the breakfast was the main attraction, but it was heartwarming to see that the Hearty Breakfast Eater is not an endangered animal, in spite of the insidious attempts of some hotels and guesthouses (thankfully none locally) to foist the continental breakfast on us.

More visitors arrived as the morning wore on, in time for elevenses, lunch, or afternoon tea, good trade for the dining room at Myers Farm and good trade in the shop that sells all sorts of souvenirs. By raising money in this way the R.S.P.B. benefits the birdlife under its care even before the visitors look at the conservation displays or settle down for an afternoon's watching in the hides. There are so many ways to help in the safekeeping of our wildlife. I found myself thinking back thirty years again, to the time in 1973 when a national tree-planting scheme was in progress to try and address the problem of a seriously under-forested country in a world suddenly aware of the destruction of the rain forests across the world. 'Plant a tree in seventy-three' was the slogan, and I did, a small sapling of alder buckthorn which I planted under the direction of John Wilson, the warden, in the peaty black soil not far from where the entrance gate to the Reserve was in those days. In unofficial circles the slogan of the day continued 'Plant some more in seventy-four', whilst the more cynical individuals added 'Lucky if they're alive in seventy-five!'

With this in mind I went to see if my tree was still there, and, happily, there it was, still flourishing thirty years later at the edge of the little brook, but now about fifteen feet high and thickened out into a well-formed bush. Wood from this species of tree used to have a wide variety of uses, including the manufacture of explosives, the making of dyes, the fashioning of pea sticks and meat skewers, and, inevitably, in medicine as a purgative. It is little used in a practical way now, in our Brave New World of plastics and manufactured chemicals, but it's always there if we ever need it, and just the look of it, a native tree in its natural habitat, is enough to gladden the heart.

The tree grows close to where the old hut used to stand, decades ago, the place where tickets were sold to visitors along with such few items of ornithological merchandise as were available. What a difference from today, when there is so much more for visitors to spend their money on and there are improved facilities for them to enjoy, and it is right that this is so. There is still much tree-planting to be done, there are ditches to clear and paths to be maintained, there is still the custodianship of the countryside now fallen on our shoulders and needing constant vigilance.

7 August

Large numbers of young pheasants, newly-released from the rearing pens, stand about in groups or shamble along the lanes as if uncertain of what to do or where to go, with few or no older birds to show the way. Without the leadership and guidance of an older generation, like the young of humans, they blunder about and get into difficulty. Unlike humans these days, the pheasants are bred merely for cannon fodder, so to speak, and it doesn't matter if they fail to learn the finer points of survival, as their chief reason for being is to succumb, not to survive.

My own pheasants, meanwhile, continue to thrive. True, we lost Hatty and her late clutch of eggs, now eaten by whatever rat, stoat or crow found them unguarded, but Hetty's two young are doing very well, still keeping their mother company but also straying away from her frequently. The young cock is growing more rapidly than his sister. Both run in my direction when they see me, their strong legs hurling them forward so that they have a passing resemblance to their small, fast-running dinosaur ancestors.

8 August

A change seems to take place in the summer season long before it ends, a change observable somewhere between the end of the first week in August and the middle of the month. This year it has been apparent this morning. It is hard to say precisely what that change is and how it is felt, but it is as if the pulse changes in the very life force which drives everything. The weather is the same as yesterday, the temperature seems no different, warm and humid, and the summer birds are still with us, though some of them not for long. There was condensation on the windows this morning for the first time in many weeks, and the swallows have started gathering on the wires, a couple of dozen at a time.

All the birds are responding to this change of mood, becoming more active after the relative ease of the long summer afternoons. They crowd in front of the house as if rehearsing their winter feeding behaviour or making some point about it being time the feeding tables were put out again. The magpie family came, and the woodpigeons, then a jackdaw and a greenfinch. There were more chaffinches about than there have been for a while. As we weeded our herb border this morning and turned over the soil, a family of marsh tits came to watch the work in progress, and of course a perky robin hopped about stamping his authority on this highly desirable feeding ground. Even a willow warbler came to sit on the top rail of a garden bench then looked for insects in the bushes close by. The needs of the birds are different now, with the breeding season over for most birds and their young fully fledged and taking care of themselves at last. The new emphasis is on looking after number one, on beginning the process of fattening up for the leaner season ahead, or in the case of the migrant birds, for the long journey south. It is fascinating watching the spotted flycatcher at the edge of Eaves Wood, flying out from its perch, catching an insect on the wing at the end of its aerial loop and returning to the same twig. It is the last summer visitor to come to us, arriving at the end of May or even in early June, and it is the first to go, usually leaving even before the swifts sometime later this month.

11 August

The roe deer have entered their rutting season. This morning our buck was chasing a doe round the garden. The air was clear after rain and carried well the music of the peal of bells at Saint John's Church three fields away. An answering call came in the ringing laughter of a green woodpecker, which was calling in my wood all morning. It is a bird more often heard than seen, delivering his clarion call in the secret depths of the woods, a call obviously to his own kind but somehow also a call to arms for all of us, a call that mocks us for neglecting the joy of life and dwelling on our difficulties.

Our homes are symbols of security in our lives. Safe behind four walls we have the leisure to muse upon the follies of the world outside. Yet too much sedentary contemplation is bad for us, and we all respond to these calls to get out into the fresh air and look around us. There are so many other signs that lead us on, the deer and the woodpecker this morning for example, or the red bee on a knapweed flower, or the scent of marjoram, mint and rosemary just outside our front door. Impossible to resist the call to walk round the village admiring the riot of colour in every garden. Rows of sunflowers and scarlet-flowered runner beans. Clusters of roses: red, white, cream and yellow. Red geraniums, coral-coloured montbretias and radiant fuchsias of crimson and purple. Banks of pink hydrangeas like clouds of candyfloss;

nasturtiums of terracotta and yellow ochre. Staghorn trees with purple, poker-like flower spikes, and creamy-white Russian vines smothering trees, hedges, barns and cottage roofs.

21 August

After we had been absent in the south for a week, Silverdale seemed to welcome us on our return, even though it was after midnight before we got back to the village at the end of a long journey. A fox stood inquisitively at the roadside, not moving as we drove past him. Our roe deer and her kid stood in the middle of Red Bridge Lane making us slow almost to a halt before they lept the stone walls effortlessly. Even the kid's legs are strong enough now to send him flying over what would have been an insuperable obstacle a month or so ago. As we pulled up in front of the house, owls hooted in the trees, and a round moon with a huge halo hung above the wood. The cooler nights mean a heavy dew on the grass in the mornings, and so it was today, the lawns decked with glittering cobwebs, but the sun was out later to clear away the vapours of the night. Dragonflies swept grandly across the garden, graceful yet primeval creatures, coming to rest on the wall above the herb border, reminding me as they always do of some sort of exotic bronze jewellery. They and the blaze of golden rod are tokens of late summer. The swifts have gone, and we shall not see them again until next May.

23 August

Just as the youthful urgency of spring gave way to the calm maturity of summer, so now summer plenty turns into the fruitfulness of autumn. Scarcely a time to be thinking of baby birds, yet this morning an unfamiliar hen pheasant came into the garden with three small chicks that can be no more than a fortnight old at most. Perhaps she was the pheasant that had the well-concealed but unsuccessful nest of ten eggs in the wood some weeks ago. Perhaps after that failure she went away and tried again, with the results we now can see. It may be that she started her breeding season late because she was a chick herself only last season and has only recently felt the desire to breed. She seemed to know where to come for food, but was hesitant about bringing her chicks until I had left the scene. Cedric came to stand by the new brood, so I suppose he must accept them as his.

Meanwhile Hetty's two youngsters are as big as she is, at least the hen chick is; the cock is larger, with a good red wattle developing behind the eye, and brandy-coloured body feathers, with a wine-red rump the model of his father's. When the younger family went off to safety, Cedric joined this well-established group and led them off for an afternoon at the edge of our wood where it meets the sheepfield. There I found them later on, enjoying the shade in the afternoon sun right by the boundary where fresh, cool water wells up from the rock and runs away in an infant stream, by the side of which the wily old pheasant knows that he and his kin will be undisturbed, with fresh drinking water to hand, good foraging in the grass and good cover to slip into should they need it. Here the young learn foraging skills and other principals of survival. The seclusion is total. Tall oaks tower over the hazel and buckthorn. Gnarled roots of oak and ash writhe and twist round boulders covered in moss and ivy and sprouting ferns from the crevices. A tangled honeysuckle scrambles up the bare lattice of thick, woody stems of dead ivy which still clings to an old cherry tree, itself at the end of its useful life, choked half to death and having only a few leaf-bearing twigs at the top. The yellow flowers of the honeysuckle are now over, all but one, the rest having turned into clusters of red berries. As yet only a very few leaves are turning, with just one now and then to slip and rustle as it falls in the silence. High above the canopy of leaves an unseen buzzard mewed its enjoyment of the sunlit skies. In its way it was an idyll, perhaps for the pheasants and certainly for me as I wandered past them and left them alone.

25 August

The crop of hazel nuts is looking promising, and there will be plenty of acorns for the birds later on. The damsons are ripening on their twisted branches, blue-black with a mealy bloom. The grass still sparkling with dew-drenched cobwebs every morning, and in the evening a thick white mist forms over Hawes Water and down the valley. The birds have been crowding round the front of the house at daybreak and well into the morning. Normally I don't bring the bird tables out of the shed until October, but 'by popular request' as they used to say in the theatres, I have started putting out food. This had the immediate effect of attracting those birds that haven't been close to the house all summer, such as the nuthatch.

Nevertheless we have been enjoying a succession of gloriously sunny afternoons, as if August is determined to reaffirm its identity as a summer month, not one that is a mere prelude to autumn. Now, in the middle of the day, the toiler in the garden is assailed by the heat, and any serious work is best done in the early morning or the evening, when it is cooler.

In the wood the stillness of summer remains, with just the lightest of breezes lifting the leaves here and there, more of a caress than a current of air. The birds, which were so eager for food in the cool of the morning, disappear in the afternoon, with only goldfinches active in the heat, marvellous creatures of red, black, gold and buff, flitting from one clump of thistles to another. A stray gasp of air ruffles the shock-headed thistles now and then, detaching fragments of thistledown that go drifting along the lanes, more vagabond weeds for the determined gardener to deplore. We are encouraged to see living things in terms of harm or benefit to ourselves, and thus lose the sense of wonder and admiration that is essential to a proper understanding of the world and our place in it. When we were children, watching thistledown drifting across the summer skies, we used to call the light, floating miracles of seed-construction 'fairies', so delicate and ethereal they seemed. We were right to express our instinctive veneration of the mysteries of nature in this way, and when one air-borne seed drifted towards us and landed on an outstretched hand as if by its own will, we felt ourselves in the presence of natural magic.

31 August

A mere handful of black-headed gulls are left at Leighton Moss, far less distraction for the other birds – and for the birdwatchers, a few of which were about today, peering out from the hides at whatever offered itself for observation in this quiet time after the breeding season and before the autumn migrations begin in earnest. There were not so many ducks about today, just a few shoveler, some teal and a vociferous mallard compensating for the general silence of the rest of duck-kind. There were, though, a lot of swallows and martins passing to and fro across the open water. They are feeding themselves up, and soon this seemingly endless activity will cease as these well-loved summer visitors leave on their long and perilous journey across sea and desert to their winter quarters in Africa.

There was interest in the shape of two cormorants swimming, looking like snakes with their bodies three-quarters submerged and sometimes just their heads and long, sinuous necks above the water. When they rested on the wooden posts sticking out of the water the white-cheeked adult preened then stuck his head under his wing, while his juvenile companion held his wings out to dry in typical fashion. Like ragged banners the wings of cormorants proclaim the ancient ancestry of the species, and the general shape of the bird suggests something far older than history, something primeval.

A bird which always seems to me to have a similar primeval appearance is the heron, with its long legs, yellow beak and long, flexible neck. We were lucky today in having one just outside the hide, where it was taking advantage of an area cleared of reeds to stand on sentry duty, watching for eels or small fish at the waterside. The grey and white plumage, black shoulder patches and black head and throat markings are so familiar, even to the casual birdwatcher, yet there is always the same interest when one of these birds appears. High stepping, methodical, patient, statuesque, the heron is not at all ungainly; rather it is the epitome of the grace and power in nature. The only loss of dignity occurs when a catch is made, particularly if it is an eel, which it often is. Then the contortions and writhings that go on before the prey is subdued enough to be swallowed are a comical sight.

September

1 September
'September is different from all other months. It is more magical'. So wrote Katherine Mansfield in 1921. Though born and brought up in New Zealand, where September is a spring month, she came to England to further her career as a writer, and her words were set down in praise of the September of the northern hemisphere, a month where the warmth of summer lingers yet the soft and gentle decay of early autumn becomes unmistakable after a few days.

For a fair-weather walker such as myself there is no time to lose, and today we found ourselves on the footpath from Hollins Lane through Fleagarth Wood, a piece of ancient woodland never entirely cleared and full of a diversity of tree species growing out of extensive tracts of limestone pavement, much of which appears above ground as large slabs of grey rock riven with fissures and runnels. Huge, serpentine tree roots clasp the rock and run over it like a lava flow solidified. It is as if the trees are stuck to the rock rather than growing out of it. The groves of venerable yews, particularly, hold on with a time-hardened tenacity. The sun cuts through their dense branches far less successfully, and the yews form a dark and secret heart to the old wood. The bright yew berries contrast strongly with the dark green needle-shaped leaves. Here and there sunlight shines through these opaque red fruit making them glow like gemstones.

We came out of the dappled shade into bright light where the steep hillside looks out over marshland and level fields towards Warton Crag and the sea. This is another unforgettable sight of the Silverdale peninsula, the tree-clad Crag, the bird-haunted pastures, the vast expanse of naked sands at low tide, the fast flowing water running up the channels when the tide has turned, the sea marsh curiously patterned with creeks and salt pools, vaguely suggestive of an Elizabethan knot garden. Here on the hillside fragile harebells trembled in the sea breeze, but it was so quiet we could hear the chirp of grasshoppers and the cracking in the sun of the hard, sharp-pointed gorse pods. A pair of crows flew high over the marsh, croaking softly to each other in a reassuring way. Not all crow calls are harsh-sounding; some are clearly conversational, perhaps even terms of endearment. Below them a couple of hikers murmured to one another in a similar fashion as they crossed the embanked causeway from Crag Foot to Brown's Point. Even the two-coach train from Barrow to Lancaster passed across the marsh with a muted sound, as if scarcely daring to disturb the peace of this special place.

A perfect scene in late summer, but nothing lasts forever, and the summer heat itself was ripening the berries on the hawthorn bushes, an unmistakable sign of the changing of the season. If autumn hasn't begun, it is waiting in the wings. High in the sky, in broad daylight, a fragment of pale moon hung like a slice of washed-out lemon left over from a summer party. We turned up Heald Brow and walked back to Hollins Lane at Hazelwood Hall.

2 September
I spent some time cutting down blackthorn, wild rose and other bushes which were threatening to topple the stones from a wall, invade the greenhouse and block light from my walnut tree, which however is holding its own in spite of the competition and the shallowness of the soil in our rocky garden. Thinning trees in the wood is not a task I enjoy, though the resulting increase in woodland flowers and insects is gratifying. I'd far rather be planting them, as I did with the walnut, as well as a holm oak, a juniper and a couple of silver birches, all of which are flourishing. The mulberry bush I planted is not quite so vigorous, but it is a scion of a noble house, so to speak, being a cutting taken from a centuries-old mulberry tree planted in the time of James the First, and it continues to make moderate progress every year.

I gathered together all the brushwood and burned it. The smoke and hot air from the bonfire attracted a large flock of black-headed gulls, about two hundred of them, which appeared as if from nowhere, flying frantically to and fro high above the flames, snapping up the insects disturbed by the fire. The gulls see the smoke from a distance and converge on it, knowing from experience that there will be a worthwhile concentration of insects there, but one wonders where do all the insects come from in these circumstances?

The fire itself surely disturbs very few of them in its immediate neighbour-hood, so are they insects already in the air, and if so why are *they* drawn to the smoke?

A buzzard came over, circling in its leisurely way ever closer to the scene of feverish activity. Perhaps there was a chance of seizing an unwary member of the gull flock as it concentrated on the insect feast, thus making its own substantial meal for the day. Though it may have been more interested in the warm air, being of all British birds the one most at home in rising ther-mal currents. In any case the gulls vanished as the buzzard approached. The sky was empty of them in seconds, leaving only the buzzard itself and three or four swallows which had also been hawking for insects in the smoke. They now turned their attention to the free-wheeling predator, and being more confident in their own powers of evasive flight than the gulls, began to harry the buzzard until it lost interest in the goings-on and continued its aerial sauntering over Eaves Wood in the direction of Arnside Knott. Within the minute the gulls had returned to pick up where they had left off, taking advantage as before of the upward funnelling of insects by the rising heat and smoke.

3 September

At dusk a hedgehog shuffled through the flower border, making the usual hedgehog noises as he went, such as rustling leaves and treading on twigs which snapped under him. Hedgehogs are often heard before they are seen. This one was making slow progress because he was snuffling after slugs and snails. A youngster of this year and not quite fully grown, he was still well able to look after himself, and will fatten up well before going into hiberna-tion, unlike the young of later litters which scarcely have time to grow suf-ficiently before bad weather is upon them.

Nearby a thrush was also dining on snails, tapping them against a stone to break their shells. An answering tapping noise came from something up in an oak. It turned out to be a nuthatch examining a branch for hidden grubs. It ran mouselike down the trunk of the tree, headfirst.

5 September

The Anglo-Saxons called this the Barley-Month, an indication of how vital a successful harvest was to them. Of course not only humans scrutinise the crops keenly for signs of dearth or plenty. A woodpigeon came today to test the elderberries in the garden, and spent time in the bush sampling the crop. He is also keeping his eye on the acorns, which look like being exceptionally abundant this year. The jays have been taking an interest in them for some time. Prompted by their prudent ways, I went to inspect the elder, damson and bramble bushes myself, but found only the blackberries ready.

I could scarcely miss them, because I was continuing the work with hook and pruning saw, cutting back invasive plants. I had good need of my thick leather gardening gloves to protect myself from the alliance of nettle, bramble and thorn. When one is cut and dragged out, somehow it whips at its assailant, bringing its companions into the fray. Stings and scratches are hard to avoid in such circumstances.

6 September

As I had half expected, the three new pheasant chicks soon went down to one which has also succumbed since. They hide at night in long grass and other ground cover, and don't take to roosting in trees for some time, even after they have learned to fly. The mortality rate among young birds is very high, which is why small birds such as wrens and blue tits have such large broods, and many species try to bring off more than one brood in a season. Pheasants are polygamous, with one cock bird espousing several hens, thus increasing his chances of at least some of his offspring surviving, though it is a case of devil take the hindmost.

But the young pheasant I have called Charlie is thriving and growing very like his father Cedric. His wine-red rump is noticeable, and he is a large bird, too, like his father. The rest of Charlie's plumage is still developing, but he is likely to be a striking bird in appearance. In behaviour he is odd. He suddenly starts, jumps, and darts to one side as if startled or chasing some invisible insect, or perhaps just prompted by some adolescent quirk, some bit of joie de vivre.

9 September

Daybreaks soon after six now. The sun has risen to thirty-five degrees by half-past eight, slanting through the trees and sending bars of light and dark across the woodland floor, touching with the same gold the beads of water on the drooping seed heads of sedges, the ripening hazel nuts, the reddening rose hips and the fine, fattening crop of plump acorns which bow down every branch and twig now in ones and twos and bunches of six or seven. The morning air is cool, and there is growing evidence that autumn is with us, though it could be said that until the swallows have gone, summer lingers yet in the tree-lined lanes and woodland margins where they are still snapping up a plentiful supply of winged insects that still congregate in the warm afternoon sun. There are butterflies about; a slow worm basks on a rock, the sun reflects brilliantly from the white walls of the house. High above a buzzard circles, and forty thousand feet above him an aeroplane is quietly unzipping the clear blue sky, leaving its twin tails of vapour like the separating edges of a sheer silk dress.

It is easy to believe, at such a time, that summer is still with us, and many of us have a need to do so for as long as we can, often long after the notion is no longer tenable. The signs are there for those who want to read them. Here and there, almost imperceptibly, the leaves are starting to change colour, showing tinges of red or yellow and turning brown at the edges.

Leaves are beginning to fall, not in flurries but one by one for the time being. It is hardly noticeable, and has been going on since early spring when the leaves first came out, but in the spring and summer months the leaf-fall is a different matter, merely a natural hazard of summer storms and the like. Now it takes on a fateful and cumulative significance. For a few more days it will be possible to ignore these signs, but soon the cry will be 'the swallows have gone!' and subsequently even the most unobservant will remark 'the leaves are turning!'

The weather seemed to mirror my feelings, for later on the sky clouded, the heat vanished and steady rain began to fall. The evening was as cool as the morning, and I lit a fire, the first of the autumn, not so much a capitulation as a comfort. Logs burned steadily in the grate and the sweet smell of woodsmoke drifted through the wood.

12 Septmember

The warm days continue. Today is cloudy but warm and humid, with a breeze blowing from the east and bringing us the benefit of an area of high pressure over the North Sea. My azalea has decided on an autumn showing this year as well as a spring one, and is putting out a handful of small bright blue flowers. The grass continues to grow of course and the lawns will need cutting for the next six to eight weeks before the growth virtually stops for the winter. Today's cut was a big one for I also took down in stages the high growth I had left all summer on the wildflower lawn. The seed is set and fallen, the roots and rhizomes are nourished and readied for next year's cowslips, moon daisies, scabious and orchids, so no harm was likely to the plants.

Not so the animal life. As the area of long grass dwindles, the creatures hiding there are crowded ever more closely together like rabbits in a corn-field. In the past I have had a slow worm fall victim to the whirling blades of the lawnmower. Today I cut down by accident a bank vole that in its attempt to escape ran in precisely the wrong direction, right under the machine. A little further on I was able to rescue a slower-moving toad because I saw it in time and was able to stop. It is impossible to avoid such sad casualties entirely, but they are few in number and the benefits of leaving parts of a large lawn to 'go wild' are immense.

14 September

A cool morning with a luminous light creating special effects as the rising sun tried to break through the bank of mist which lay along the valley. Threads of gossamer hung from the oaks or drooped from branch to branch like strings of glass beads. Sheep in silhouette stood like statues, one of them with three starlings on its back with their beaks all pointing in the same way. They were pausing in their work of picking up sheep ticks. Not far away seven rooks sat in a row on consecutive fence posts, also resting from their labours in the field, in their case gobbling up weed seeds, grubs and drowsy insects.

19 September
On the very morning that I realise the swallows have all gone, my climbing rose puts out its final pink-edged, cream-petalled flower at the top of the wall, a last defiant gesture of summer. All around it the tokens of autumn are growing increasingly obvious. The slow worms come out still, but are more slow-moving than ever. Thick clusters of acorns hang from coronas of leaves that are browning round the edges as the tree withdraws its energies from leaf production and puts them into self-perpetuation on the one hand and self-preservation on the other. Another crop, of various types of fungus, is replacing the few lingering flowers as the centre of attention. As well as the field mushrooms which are always worth looking out for, there are small, white, round puff-balls pushing through the short grass of the lawns, and ink-cap toadstools as well, with shaggy conical caps changing rapidly from white to a sort of inky sepia as they decay. All delicious, if picked at the right time and properly cooked, but the picker (and the eater) needs to beware that he has not gathered by mistake one of those species that are inedible, or worse, poisonous. These latter categories are more numerous, and include the broad, shelf-like protrusions of bracket fungus now decorating the trunks of some of the older trees, and the stinkhorn toadstool lurking in the shadier places with its foul smell and uncompromising shape.

21 September
In villages up and down the land harvest suppers are being held or are in the offing, a link with the once all-important celebrations of Harvest Home, which has not the significance now that it once had, even in the countryside. Michaelmas Fairs, once famous throughout the land, are now forgotten. Yet the gathering and garnering which for centuries prompted such festivals were part of an age-old force which still drives wild creatures to adopt a strategy for survival in the coming months and follow the course of action which best suits them. Some migrate, some hibernate, some gather in stores of food and others merely fatten themselves up and hope for the best. Hedgehogs are on the prowl, feasting on beetles, worms and slugs before retiring to their winter quarters. Slow worms are spending longer in their underground chambers, and though wood mice and bank voles are running over the rocks in broad daylight, it is only because they feel a sense of urgency, as the days grow shorter. These are the busiest of animals as they store up seeds, nuts and berries in secret places beneath the surface of the limestone.

However the birds are the most noticeable. The ones remaining all belong to the 'live to eat and hope to live' school of survival, apart from jays that are unlike most birds in that they store their food. Blue tits and great tits cluster round the peanuts, or compete for space at a cylinder of fat that also hangs from the bird table. Coal tits concentrate on mixed seed, while marsh tits are happy with the tiny black niger seeds which they take from the small holes in a special holder.

Nuthatches, chaffinches and collared doves all join in the general free for all on the table top, where kitchen scraps and breadcrumbs add a little variety to the wild bird seed. The keenest attention, however, is reserved for a dispenser full of sunflower hearts, which all small birds devour eagerly. Greenfinches especially are attracted to them, and it has been a joy to watch a party of four or five goldfinches at a time flocking round the table.

Our robin eats where he pleases, but is inordinately fond of live meal-worms and has grown tame enough to wait for my appearance then fly down to take the live food as I put it on the table for him. If another robin turns up, a fight for possession of this highly desirable feeding station takes place. I watched such a fight today, one robin flat on its back on the ground with its wings spread out while the other stood over it in unmistakable triumph. Now is the season when robins become more territorial than ever, when pairs split up and fight one another for the piece of ground they once shared, especially where the feeding is good even if there is plenty for all comers. Thus robins become solitary in the autumn for just a few months, largely it would seem because of the great imperative, the need to find food and stay alive. Yet a pair of robins will be the earliest birds in the garden to pair up again in advance of the breeding season, joining their respective territories and defending them together, both sexes equally combative, as early as January or sometimes even December. How ironic it is that round about Christmas time robins are featuring in solitary splendour on snowy Christmas cards, just the time when they are getting together again. Here and now it is much more likely, as I also saw today, to see a single robin in close company with a wren, though for what reason it has yet to be established. Certainly the curious occurrence of these two different species being seen close to one another on many occasions has been observed for centuries, with the result that for a long time it was thought that they were female and male of one species, 'jenny wren' the mate of 'cock robin'.

26 September
We watched a roe deer and her fawn, eating acorns on our lawn. The kid is now about four months old, and half grown, no longer the striped, gangling, vulnerable creature it was when it was born in the wood back in the middle of May. It has spent the summer opposite us in Letter Box Field, hiding in the long grass by day and moving about in its mother's company by night. It is now no longer left on its own but is the doe's constant companion, which is what it will remain until next April.

October

1 October

The 'Season of mists and mellow fruitfulness' of Keats's beloved poem is upon us. Layers of mist rise and lie along the valley morning and evening. There are sunny days and glorious vermilion sunsets. There was a very heavy mist this morning, out of the top of which Trowbarrow loomed, looking twice as high as usual, like a great cliff in a lost world, one massive, grey, flat face, with equally flat silhouettes of trees surrounding and tributary walls running up towards it from the valley bottom. There was a hint of light at half past six, and daylight was growing at seven o'clock, under a heavy canopy of mist and cloud. As a robin sang and a crow called at the break of day, an owl hooted on its way to roost. With twelve hours of darkness already, the owls have their own richness of autumn harvest, with so many of the summer litters of small mammals now fully-grown and busy in their preparations for winter.

It might be supposed that the owls have a hand in the numbers of dead shrews to be found at this time of year on woodland walks, but the presence of the little carcasses has nothing to do with owls, which hold on to anything they catch and seldom if ever waste food. Shrews are pugnacious little creatures, the most ferocious animal on earth for its size, it has been said, if such comparisons mean anything. Certainly when two shrews meet there is often a fight, and it has long been thought that these autumn casualties are the result of such clashes.

I remember long ago hearing a commotion just outside my living room window and, on going out to investigate, was confronted with the sight of a shrew, upright and indignant, gibbering abuse at its antagonist, which in this case was not another shrew but a cat, that enemy of all small birds and mammals. The cat was of course many times bigger than the shrew, which it had cornered and could easily have killed at any time with one swipe of its claws, but it was being held in check by the sheer, unremitting shrill fury of the tiny rodent. I don't think I have come across a better example of getting your own way, or at least of getting out of scrapes, by making a lot of blustering noise.

Having hastily removed the cat I carefully gathered up the shrew in an empty jam jar and set it at liberty in a safe place, but was I thanked for my pains? Not at all! The shrew carried on shrieking, at me now and not the cat, until I had set it free and it had disappeared into some long grass. Shrews live short lives, and have a lot of hatred to pack into that brief space, it would seem. The brevity of their lifespan, only about fourteen months, is probably the real reason for the shrew carnage we encounter on our autumn walks. All born at roughly the same time in the spring or summer, they are all dying of old age in the autumn of the following year.

2 October

Each morning the thick mist is pierced by the sun, which comes slanting into the wood, touching the yellow seed-heads of woodland grasses to make a floor of gold. In this golden early light I watched a pair of speckled wood butterflies performing a circular aerial dance together. Not as colourful, or as large, as some of the more colourful species, the speckled wood is nevertheless a dainty, delicately marked insect, wholly typical of limestone woodland. Round and round in one particular shaft of sunlight went this couple, a ball of fragile but intense movement. They were blissfully ignorant of fruition, decay, decline and dissolution, of the harsh winds of winter and the imminent termination of their light-filled summer existence. They had no thought of the intractable issues of life and death which never cease to fascinate – and appall – the human mind, that same mind which sometimes yearns to put its understanding on one side and live just for the tumbling moment, dancing in the sunlight like the butterflies.

3 October

The first rain for some time fell last night and with it came high winds, resulting in the first fall of leaf of any significance, a good scattering of leaves on the lawns and a steadily augmenting carpet of them glistening on the woodland floor. The black and spotted palmate leaves of sycamore are the least attractive among them, though fortunately there are not too many of those. Much more appealing are the dainty, triangular, butter-yellow leaves of birch with saw-tooth edges, the green-gold oak leaves with their equally distinctive lobed shape, and the seven-lobed ash leaves, yellowing at the base but still green higher up though all spotted with the marks of the changing season. The slanting sun gives the rough bark of the oaks a silvered look, and the crown of leaves a curious rusty red.

6 October
The leaves are falling, small mammals are busy assembling their winter store of nuts and berries, and other birds and animals are fattening themselves as best they can, but in the gardens of the village there is a continued flowering and fruiting, a process which is both a completion of the summer's work and a prolongation of it. The brilliant sunshine is swelling fat yellow pumpkins and thick green marrows in vegetable gardens. Long runner beans hang from the climbing vines twined round bamboo sticks, side by side with scarlet bean flowers still showing. Plump and spiky artichokes are sporting thistle-like tufts of blue flowers. In the flower gardens there are Michaelmas daisies, Chinese lanterns, sweet-smelling rambler roses, sweet peas of white and red, dahlias of pure white or rich burgundy, nasturtiums of fire-red, egg yellow, orange and wine colours, hosts of blooms. Gardens full of produce, testifying to all the hard work and loving care lavished on them these many months. In my own garden a presumptuous primula is flowering, months too early – or too late, depending on which way you look at it.

8 October
 One year out of two we have a good crop of acorns. This year is a year of plenty, and it is instructive to see how greatly the crop is valued by all manner of creatures, even if mankind less appreciates it these days. It wasn't always so. Thomas Tusser, the Elizabethan writer and observer of farming and nature, in his book 'Five Hundred Points of Good Husbandry', published in 1573, emphasises the importance of acorns as a crop for fattening hogs, and for the continuance of good forestry. Now we are much more likely to watch woodpigeons gorging themselves on acorns, rather than pigs.
  Our crop of acorns is especially good on the two oaks flanking our drive. I watched some woodpigeons at work on them this morning, and a pair of jays filling their crops and beaks with up to a dozen acorns at a time then carrying them off to a hiding place, sometimes only a few yards away on the lawns, but often across the fields and near the edge of a wood. Like many other creatures, including a dog with his bone, jays bury surplus food at a time of plenty, and almost invariably find what they have hidden when food is scarce in the depths of winter, even under snow which we might have thought made searching for secret larders impossible. Those few stores of acorns which the jay fails to find sprout in the spring and stand a chance of becoming the next generation of oaks. It is thought that by this means the jay was one of the main agents in the spread of oakwoods, especially on

rising ground where the spread of oaks by fallen or wind blown seed would be less likely.

There was also a grey squirrel making his selection, and a roe deer on the lawn feeding on the plentiful supply. Where some acorns had fallen on the drive and been crushed under the wheels of our car, magpies came to feed on the fragments, as did various members of the pheasant clan. Mice and voles come under cover of darkness, and sometimes in broad daylight, to take their share and scamper off with it to their many dens and storerooms beneath the limestone pavement. When I first came to live here I thought to sweep the drive clear of these crushed acorns, thereby upholding suburban values, I suppose, but illness prevented me from carrying out the plan. What delights would have been denied by an excess of zeal!

11 October
As the leaves continue to tumble from the taller trees, singly or in sudden, spectacular showers as circumstances dictate, the smaller trees, easily overlooked before in a garden or on a country walk, start to attract our attention. Not those lesser trees such as hawthorn, hazel and elder, which with their distinctive leaves, showy blossom, conspicuous fruits, or all three, draw attention to themselves almost all year round, but the unobtrusive, bushy trees which now, because of a singular tenacity of leaf or unusual bright berry, rival the more familiar species.

One of these is the single purging buckthorn, about sixteen feet high, which in our garden holds its own in the shadow of a cherry, an oak and a hawthorn. In the spring its leaves come out a little later than those of its neighbours but now it is holding on to them as they lose theirs, and at the same time bearing clusters of glossy black berries which shine like polished ebony in the autumn sunlight. The buckthorns are so called because of their thorny twigs, which are said to bear a resemblance to the antlers of a roebuck. Long ago buckthorn wood was one of those timbers deemed good for making charcoal, and the berries were used to make dyes, but the most significant use of the tree long remained in the use of the juice of its berries as a powerful, even violent, purgative, hence its name.

Another tree of what might be called a modest, retiring disposition is the spindle, of which there are several in the wood and one handsome specimen by our front gate. It grows only as high as about twenty feet, bears inconspicuous flowers and has thin, spindly stems, though that is not why it bears the name of spindle tree. Its wood is hard and durable and was used to make pegs, skewers and other domestic utensils, especially the spindles used by, typically, the unmarried girls or 'spinsters' in that commonest of household activities, the spinning of wool. The powdered leaves were used as a dust to keep lice from the hair and skin of children, and the fruits were used as an emetic. It is these four-lobed, bright red fruits or seed pods which are such a notable feature just now.

The bird cherry differs from the buckthorn and the spindle by having beautiful, heavily scented flower spikes in the spring, but the rest of the time it is easily overlooked and, unlike its flowers, the fruit have no appeal to humans, having a bitter taste which the birds don't mind. In my experience this tree attracts all sorts of little birds all year round, not just when there are berries to be eaten, and they always seem to find something to eat there which is invisible to the human eye, whether it be tiny insects or the bark itself that acts as some sort of medicine. The bark contains tannin, and used to provide both a sedative for stomach disorders and as a flavouring for alcohol. We may think of people in past centuries as woefully lacking in life's refinements, but there was no lack of essential materials or ready availability of effective herbal remedies. And with the added advantage that whereas we have to put up with ugly factories to ensure a steady supply of the chemicals we regard as indispensable to our way of life, our ancestors could benefit from a simple bush growing in a hedgerow, which in itself is decorative and provides a constant procession of some of the most appealing of garden visitors, such as the pair of goldcrests which I watched today in one of our bird cherries. It is also known as the golden-crested wren, because it is so small, even smaller than our familiar garden wren in fact, though not a close relation and much less likely to be seen because it keeps mainly to conifer woods. When the goldcrest pair went away, an ordinary wren appeared in their place, just as active, only slightly larger, with plumage less colourful but no less beautiful in its own way. He paused long enough to throw out his short, loud, clear song, which has such great appeal for the human ear, especially coming from such a tiny frame. Wordsworth, hearing the song of a wren at Furness Abbey, was moved to write:

> So sweetly 'mid the gloom the invisible bird
> Sang to itself that there I could have made
> My dwelling place and lived for ever there.

18 October
The garden was white over with the first frost of autumn. The last of the marigolds still stood bravely with their sugar coating of ice crystals, and the leaves on the fig tree on our south-facing wall, often the first to succumb, were unharmed. The sun came out and the frost melted, shivering from the trees like drops of silver. Along the lanes the haw leaves are turning from green to red-brown and dropping to the hedge bottoms where they lie like an accumulation of rust flakes. The thinning of the leaves throws into relief the creeping plants that all summer have been making their way towards the sun and now produce a spectacular finish to their season. Along Ford Lane the long creepers of bryony are now woody with age, and having held their own against the toughest weeds have emerged triumphant in a bush or along a fence rail, setting out their pedlar's pack of glossy scarlet berries like

so many ropes of coral beads. On Waterslack Lane the wild clematis, usually known as traveller's joy, is a fine sight just now. All summer it has twined its way through the dense vegetation of the hedges, twisting its leaf stems as tendrils round the branches of the host trees and emerging at the outermost edges to flower, and now to produce its feather-like seed clusters, each seed bearing its own long, thin, waving plume, the mass of them festooning the hedge like long, flowing, grey hair, from which the plant gets its other name of old man's beard. An appropriate autumnal name, and though the frost melted quickly this morning, the old man's beard continued to give the illusion of it.

29 October

A week of mixed weather with a fair amount of rain. Wet this morning, clearing later but with grey skies all day. A fairy ring of grey mushrooms on the lawn: a sombre enchantment, and to complete the mood, a skein of grey geese tiny against the thick cloud high up, uttering those evocative calls which never fail to attract human attention. All the wild, free lonely places we have ever known seem to be wrapped up in that one haunting cry.

30 October

I took down the empty nest box where the blue tits reared their young again this year, and examined the nest material, a mass of leaves, sheep's wool and dried grasses, with moss and feathers added to the structure and a cup lined with hair and finer grass. A little trampled now after being occupied by a restless, demanding brood of growing nestlings, but still a marvellous work of nature to behold. The number of hours the birds had taken to construct it – and now I simply threw it away! Next year the birds will want to start again with new materials, not old ones which might be infested with insect parasites which spend the winter in the cosy comfort of the old nest. I cleaned the box and left it drying in the sun before fixing it up again outside the kitchen window.

31 October

Another frost. Overnight the leaves on our fig tree have blackened and fallen, so literally as well as metaphorically our fig leaves have gone, and there is no longer any pretence of continued fine weather. Summer clothes have been put away. Everything is shutting down.

Nevertheless late autumn has its consolations. Though elder and bird cherry are now bare, the lilac bush is still green and the tints of the remaining leaves on other trees continue to have appeal. Ash trees are still leafy and mostly green, hazels are a sort of rusty green, oaks are a range of colours from green-brown to blazing gold, and a horse chestnut in the village still bears its large palmate leaves which are now a pure yellow. Reds, yellows, russets, browns: the colours are of earth and fire. The stored sunlight of the year is burning itself out through the leaves, many of which now form deep drifts in the wood. Kicking up the leaf-drifts just as in childhood days long gone is a temptation impossible to resist.

There were other places where the leaves had to be swept up, and there was firewood to be brought down from the log mountain in the wood to augment the log pile just in front of the house. The wood is now well seasoned, and in the evenings now the sweet-smelling wood smoke curls up from our chimney from the darkening skies.

To the English people of more than a thousand years ago this was the Wine Month, a time for the laying down of all sorts of provisions for the winter. It remains a time of home brewing and wine making, of pickling, preserving and jam making. When I was a boy our kitchen and back-kitchen were full of the heat and steam and smells of these autumn activities. Wonderful jams were produced from fruit that was given to us or came free from the hedgerow. Blackberry and apple featured strongly, and marrow and apple was probably my favourite. There was a heady aroma from the making and bottling of wine, particularly the strong-tasting peapod and parsnip which made an inquisitive small boy wrinkle his nose in distaste, and the queen of wines, the potent elderberry. This year, right at the end of the wine-month, I picked sloes from the bushes in our garden and made sloe gin. It's a simple enough recipe: equal measures by volume of one third sloes, sugar and gin. Prick the sloes with a needle, add the sugar and gin. Keep for at least six months, turning the bottle from time to time. At its best at about eight years. I set aside one bottle for my grand-daughter's sixteenth birthday, eight years from now.

Jenny Brown's Point from Warton Crag

November

> '*No shade, no shine, no butterflies, no bees,*
> *No fruits, no flowers, no leaves, no birds, - November!*'

Thus wrote the poet Thomas Hood, and many of us echo his sentiments. There is something about the very name 'November' which strikes a chill. The days are shortening noticeably, the nights are long and dark, and the situation is not going to improve for the best part of two months. The weather will only get worse with no significant improvement until February. The Anglo-Saxons called this the Wind Month, because of the gales which they knew would come, and, even more chillingly, the Blood Month. It was a time for them to slaughter much of the livestock and salt down the carcasses to provide food for what they knew would be a long, hard winter, and because in any case there would not be enough fodder for all the beasts. The dark nights and the killing were not without the very real compensations of good food and good company indoors beside the fires. Thomas Tusser wrote, over four hundred years ago:

> *At Hallontide, slaughter time entereth in,*
> *and then doth the Husbandman's feasting begin.*

There is plenty of feasting going on in our garden, where the acorn crop is still attracting daily visitors, this morning a roe deer. Little birds flocked to the two bird tables, eager for whatever was put out for them. Though the pheasant clan has deserted the garden, the hens and their offspring, the old patriarch, Cedric, remains, as resplendent in his autumn feathers as he was in the spring ones. He has an occasional male companion but no more. Cock pheasants form their bachelor parties now for the winter season, and then hens go about in, well, hen parties. Those Christmas cards with pictures of pheasants in the snow are all very well if they show two cock birds, but are likely to be ornithologically inaccurate if they depict a cock and a hen. These winter alliances can be quite firm and enduring, though a lot of pheasants seem to wander about on their own for much of the time. It is a time of dispersal. They can be seen everywhere: searching along the hedge bottoms for seeds, grubs and insects, standing in the middle of a field in proud possession, or as if in thought at the responsibilities of land ownership. They stand in garden gateways looking at people's lawns and flower borders with a knowledgeable air. They wander along the lanes absent-mindedly, courting disaster from passing traffic. I have even seen a cock pheasant standing at the edge of the platform at Silverdale Railway Station at nine o'clock in the morning, looking for all the world as if he were waiting for the down train from Barrow to Lancaster.

3 November
Mixed weather: rain yesterday, bright today. The rain came from the east and brings down more leaves than the wind just now. The east side of the wood is nearly bare, but the landscape in general is half bare and half leafy. Thomas Hood's assertion that there are 'no flowers' is not entirely true, because there are several sorts which can be seen just about now, the commoner ones mostly, such as daisy, dandelion and gorse, the latter putting out at least a few flowers in every month of the year, reminding us of the old saying 'When gorse is not in flower, kissing's out of season.' Nor was Hood correct in the flat statement 'no birds'. Though his negatives have a convincing and a suitable effect, based on how many folk feel at this time of year, there are always birds to be seen, for those who know where to look, and in Silverdale that is not difficult. Leighton Moss has its wintering ducks, the marshes and the sands of the Bay have more ducks, and waders alongside them. Buzzards soar in blue skies when the sun comes out, and, come rain or shine the solitary heron stalks the field edges looking for frogs and voles, or stands patiently waiting for eels and small fish in the straight-cut channels leading from the Moss down to the sea. The fields are full of grazing geese, lapwing flocks and mixed companies of rooks and jackdaws that are full of their customary vitality. If many of our summer breeding birds have gone abroad for the winter, as we would often like to do, there are visitors from abroad to take their place, and movements of species within the British Isles. Thus it is that flocks of woodpigeons appear and disappear, and the annual, and very welcome, visit of the Scandinavian thrushes takes place. Fieldfares

have arrived, flying over quite high and calling as they go. Redwings are here too, like their cousins the fieldfares travelling always in close proximity to one another, as tourists do when travelling in a foreign country. When they see a bush where there are edible berries they descend as one, and feed heartily. Haws are a favourite, but there are plenty of other berries on offer, such as the waxy-looking rose hips which as children we used to call 'itchy powder' because the hair-like inner fibres had a mild irritant effect on the skin, so were ideal for putting down the neck of your best friend.

4 November
It was light at half past six this morning. I stood in the wood, watching the leaves fall and listening to a blackbird singing briefly, well out of season. I didn't have to do anything, not think or say or do, just *be*. The leaves grow, the leaves fall, my part in the existence of the trees from which they fall is a brief custodial one. One day they will be someone else's responsibility, but it is not for me to concern myself needlessly about their future, merely enjoy them and care for them while I can.

Nearby a thrush had found a snail, and was beating it with some force against a rock to break the shell. The song thrush is a bird which has fallen on hard times, principally it would seem because so many of us are using slug pellets and other 'molluscicides', as they are called, to try and control slugs and snails in our gardens. As the song thrush depends so much on that type of food it takes in far more of the poison than other birds will, hence the decline in numbers, a situation complicated by the disappearance of snails in winter. Song thrushes are more specialised feeders than, say black-birds, and I have never seen one on my bird table, where a wide choice of seed is on offer. If left to their own devices, and not interfered with by us, I shrewdly suspect that the thrushes would be all right, because they know the sorts of places to look for hibernating snails, which cluster together in quite large groups. So if a thrush finds one snail, he knows where to come for more, and can survive the harshest weather. Not so if he is already half-poisoned before winter begins.

What then is to be done? In the long run we must learn to take better care of the natural world, and curb some of our more harmful practices. In the mean time, none of us likes to see our lettuces munched and our radishes nibbled by the ever-present slugs in our garden, but do we really want to eat food that we have grown ourselves in soil we have poisoned ourselves with mercury and other toxic agents? A simple solution is to use beer slops as I used to do when I brewed my own beer, or, if you must, buy a bottle of beer for the express purpose of mollusc destruction. Cheap lager will do, slugs have no taste and will drown contentedly in ale of any quality. Alternatively, try concentrating the pellets in one place, rather than broadcasting them across flower beds and vegetable plots. The slugs and snails will quickly find them and make straight for them. If they are contained in a homemade slug-trap the problem of disposing of the unpleasant contents, and avoiding contaminating the soil at the same time, will be solved. Such a trap can be made very easily from one of those little plastic or cardboard tubs that contain margarine, yogurt, coleslaw, bean salad and so many other grocery items these days. Clear plastic is best, from the point of view of seeing at a glance what lies inside. One or two holes cut in the sides, of a sufficient size to permit the entrance of slugs and snails, should be high enough to stop the pellets falling out. If the pot is then fixed firmly in the soil and weighted down with a stone to stop it blowing over, it is ready to attract and destroy the slow-moving but relentless devastators of our garden produce. The addition of a piece of old tile or slate will hide the glare of white plastic from view and protect it from the rain. After a suitable time the whole container can be put in the bin with household waste and the process repeated. No contaminated lettuces, no dead birds, and no doubt more than enough snails always left over to support the thrushes. You avoid paying good money for patent slug traps that have to be washed out each time you use them.

6 November

People had a good night for their fireworks last night, a mild evening after a dry day. Only after the last rocket had soared and the last banger had exploded did the rain begin to extinguish the remnants of a thousand local bonfires. In the dead of night it rained quite heavily, and the lawns were sodden this morning, but the rain passed over, the skies cleared and the sun shone, so I went for a walk in Eaves Wood, where the birds were active. A pair of jays, busy in their acorn gathering, eyed me suspiciously from the shelter of a holly bush. A pair of great spotted woodpeckers, probably the ones which came into my garden earlier, moved through the bushes as I walked along, muttering low notes of encouragement to each other.

A green woodpecker flashed across the path in front of me, disturbed at his probing in the anthills. I could see the holes his beak had made, but he hadn't had to dig deeply because the ant communities haven't entirely disappeared underground for the winter yet, and on each hill I looked at there were small numbers of ants wandering sluggishly about, seemingly lacking their usual purpose and organisation, carrying nothing back to their citadel and looking as if they were wondering what to do with themselves, like autumn holidaymakers at the seaside, trying to make use of a few hours of sunlight when all the attractions are shut up.

There is enough warmth in the air to keep some insects going for the time being, such as the ants and a fly or two, which is good for those birds that rely on them a lot, but already the death sleep is overcoming many of them, such as the drowsy crane fly that fluttered along the path in front of me. Many insects have already gone into hibernation, including the small tortoiseshell butterfly that has attached itself to the picture rail above my bed and sleeps with folded wings on a background the same colour as itself.

The path through the wood was strewn with fallen leaves forming a rich, random pattern like a mosaic, each piece of which was of a different hue and pattern.

The triangular birch leaves, tan-coloured or bright yellow, mixed with dull brown sycamore leaves, russet oak leaves, green pine needles and the leaves of smaller compass such as hawthorn, buckthorn and ivy. Still there are a few trees bearing green leaves, including one beech half-clad with them, but the overwhelming effect in the wood on those trees still with leaves to show, was of yellow gold and shining bronze this sunny autumn afternoon. The Beech Walk is carpeted uniformly with leaves of a burnished copper from the smooth-barked trees. The bristly, four-lipped seed cases have fallen, too, and lie among the leaves, shedding their flat brown seeds.

Further on, where the trees thinned out, there was a view over the fields and the grey roofs of the village of the glittering, grey blue sea. The tide was in and the big bay was filled, a permanent reminder that long ago the village had a thriving maritime life to supplement the farming economy of Silverdale. The picturesque survival of the village much as it used to be brings in tourist money these days instead.

7 November
Dry, bright and still, but colder, with a strong breeze springing up in the late morning bringing rain to mix with the sunlight to create a rainbow over Challan Hall. The birds ignored rain, wind, sun and cold alike to fly to and fro, like flurries of leaves, eager visitors to the tubes of fat and hoppers full of grain and peanuts. For centuries it has been noticed that, while larger birds remain aloof for the most part (because they are much more likely to be persecuted either for food or because they are considered a threat in some way) the smaller birds draw nearer to houses not only when the weather is bad and when it is likely to be so. The various species of tit, for example, finding it ever harder to winkle out spiders, insects and other invertebrates from their hiding places, turn to what we can provide for them. Marsh tits are the most numerous at the minute, making short work of the niger seeds which also attract goldfinches. These brightly-coloured birds spend time at the feeding ports whereas, for the most part, the tits are here and gone in a second, the exception being the great tits, which have learned from other species that it is worth spending time occupying a position so that it does not fall to somebody else.

The usual species are there, the chaffinches with their colourful plumage and combative but social behaviour, the shy, solitary, ground-loving hedge sparrow, whose latin name, 'prunella modularis', suggests a housewife diligently seeking after crumbs fallen from the table. A bullfinch appeared and sat in the bare branches of a dwarf magnolia planted in a half-barrel of wooden staves bound with iron. He was joined by a great tit, then a robin, three colourful birds together like three baubles on a surreal Christmas tree. The feathers of many species are bright and new looking after the autumn moult, none more so than this beautiful cock bullfinch, as richly coloured as a bird of the tropics. His companions of the moment left him, and went about their own business, which at this time of year is mainly feeding. He sat on until he was sure there was no danger then flew down on to the bird table to eat his fill.

16 November
Now most of the leaves are down I redouble my efforts to clear them from those places where they are a mild inconvenience, such as on the path through my wood. I find the lawnmower convenient for the job, but even in this season it pays to be vigilant, for just in time I saw a frog in front of the machine. As it hopped away I saw what a vivid green and yellow it was, a remarkable colour variation I had never seen before. It had probably delayed its hibernation because of the continuing mildness of the weather, which is encouraging so many unseasonal manifestations. Apple trees have fruit and flowers on them at the same time, my clematis is in bloom and there are fallen acorns already sprouting in the wood.

18 November
After such mild weather there was a cold wind blowing from the east today, giving us the first really cold day of the autumn and all the more reason for the tawny owl to be out hunting this evening. There he was at dusk, watching me from his tree stump as I watched a big, round moon rising over Trowbarrow at four o'clock in the afternoon, like a huge blue-veined yellow cheese in the purple sky.

20 November
The cold wind has gone and been replaced by rain, part of a whole continent of rain cloud which stretches in a broad band from Greenland to the coast of West Africa.

21 November
Wet and windy. The leaves are nearly all off the trees now. Yesterday I noticed how many leaves were still clinging to our lilac bush, but today I saw them all on the lawn, fallen in one large, yellow semi-circle around the bush.

22 November
A brilliant golden sky at eight o'clock this morning and the rising sun lighting up the highest points in the Silver Dale, the trees around Challan Hall, the church tower away across the fields. In the evenings the sun sets in a fiery tumult of the western heavens, and though it gives us little warmth at

this time of year, it reminds us that though we must expect the fog, rain and frost, the bareness of the trees, the short days and long dark nights, the sun is ever present, even when we can only see its light reflected from the moon at night, as this evening when the moon hung high above the wood, making Red Bridge Corner look like one of those nocturnal scenes by the Victorian painter, Atkinson Grimshaw. When there is no moon there are the stars in the sky, millions of distant suns showing us that darkness is an illusion.

29 November
From the brow of Stankelt Road there is a panoramic view of the vale of Leighton Moss spread out between the Heights of Heald Brow and Fleagarth on the one hand and Warton Crag, Grisedale and Cringlebarrow on the other. The acres of reed are a sort of mid-brown in colour, like bracken on a hillside. Down on the Moss itself the colours changed as the sun came out. The magic never fails: the steely blue rippling waters of the meres became the same blue as the sky and the brown reed turned the bronze of a field of ripe corn. On such a day it is a joy just to sit in one of the hides and watch the play of sun and wind on the water and the reed, irrespective of what birds are there to be seen.

But rarities never come amiss, and this morning's treat was a Slavonian Grebe, all the way from eastern Europe its name suggests, but perhaps an individual from the small Scottish breeding population. It swam not in company with its own kind but with a sort of guard of goosanders, much bigger birds, three drakes in a livery of creamy white and bottle green and two ducks in grey and chestnut. Its own plumage, orange-tawny flanks and conspicuous yellow head tufts which sweep back from the eyes in a distinctive style, has given way to the winter plumage of white neck and cheeks and dark cap or crown, but the appearance of the rarity was one of those special moments which at Leighton Moss, to the thousands of birdwatchers who come there regularly, are thankfully not at all scarce.

December

1 December

Thick, low cloud ensured that the light was dim until nine o'clock this morning. The day was dry, but with a wind blowing, suggesting rain later. Smoke gusting down from chimney pots instead of rising into the air. A pair of crows enjoying a wind-blown excursion across the fields from their wood, looking like darker clouds of smoke themselves being tossed and turned by the stiff breeze.

The wind grew stronger and the rain came on. We are in what the Anglo-Saxons called the Winter Month, with drab colours, damp in the air and on the ground, and life much less apparent in the plants and trees, but life goes on even at this supposedly dead time of year. The stinking hellebore, that striking plant with the unappealing name, is putting out green shoots already.

3 December

The rain and wind of the last couple of days died away today, leaving scattered pools and soggy patches in the corners of fields. A continuation of the mild weather we have had throughout the autumn, but there is frost ahead in a day or two, so the weather forecasters tell us. With their instruments and scientific techniques they are able to give us an accurate (though not infallible) prediction of what the weather is going to be like, but how do the birds know? The bigger birds, the jays and magpies, redoubled their efforts at the bird table, taking away food to store it safely for when the ground is hard and other food is scarce.

It was marvellously still, especially in the late afternoon when the only sounds to be heard were the going-to-bed noises made by the birds, the insistent 'pick pick' of a blackbird, the crowing of a pheasant in the wood, the 'kronk' of a heron as it flew slowly over the garden. The only human sound was that of a train rattling through the cuttings, sounding its horn to warn any lingering walkers on the crossings, then receding into the distance until the silence closed in again.

5 December

A change in temperature. Frost this morning, crisp underfoot. My two dogs snuffling in the brittle sedges after field voles, as their ancestors did before them for many tens of thousands of years. Roofs white with frost; smoke rising straight up from chimneys. Lawns and fields white over. Sheep lying down in fields, looking as though they are made out of frost themselves, reluctant to move from the frost-free patch of ground they have kept warm overnight. Birds crowding on the feeding tables even before dawn had properly broken to get at the food freshly put out. When most of them had eaten their fill, a lame starling came down on his own, separate from the rest of his flock. Hopping on one leg and tucking the useless one out of the way, the crippled bird came to the bird tables several times during the day, eager to devour what it could with the minimum of effort before another long dark night enveloped it. A bird with one injured leg can survive for quite some time, even in harsh weather. One with an injured wing is unlikely to live more than a day or two.

Later there was a partial thaw, beginning with the tops of the trees as they were touched by the first rays of the sun. Water ran down the trunks and pattered from the ends of the twigs on to the leaf litter below.

6 December

The frost continues. Only a few days ago in mild weather the fallen leaves were becoming compacted in a disagreeable sludge. Now they are brittle, well defined and stuck by the frost to the rocks, the grass and one another. The very last of the dog's mercury has been laid low; the last lingering leaves of the fig tree have finally let go. Only beds of moss stand tall, their green spikes covered in frost and looking like miniature pine forests in snow. At night the stars glitter brighter than ever in a clear sky, as if newly polished, and there is utter silence all round the house and garden, apart from the unearthly, choking scream of a vixen down by the mere. From a greater distance came the answering bark of a dog fox.

10 Decemebr

A succession of dry and sunny days, with a cold wind blowing from the north east. All leaves dried out, forming brittle, curled-up fists or flat palms patterned with dried-up veins. They are carried by the wind into drifts or tangled in the coarser woodland grasses. In the subdued light of the wood some of the birds mysteriously turn themselves into dry leaves; a robin in an oak, keeping still on the twig where he perches, resembles in the half-light a last cluster of red-brown leaves. A tree creeper runs like a wind-blown leaf up the trunk of the same tree. On Hawes Water the wind ruffles the surface of the deep, silent water but stirs nothing beneath, and the path round the edge is sheltered and quite warm where the sun shines on the white bark of birch and the flaky red trunks of yews. In the afternoon a red sun drops behind the tower of Saint John's Church away across the fields at about half past three, gilding the tree tops and filling the western sky with layers of pure blue, opal-cream, fiery gold and indigo. At night a half moon hangs over the wood and the clear sky is full of stars.

11 December

The same raw, biting wind continued to blow, over the hills and across the fields from some remote and ice-bound land. It was the sort of wind that seems to slice to the bone. Even the six proud well-wrapped walkers I saw today in the lanes of Silverdale had an extra inducement to step smartly along. The wind ruffled the reedbeds and corrugated the iron-grey meres of Leighton Moss, keeping all the birds undercover, even the ducks which kept from the open water and stood or floated at the edge of the reeds in sunny, sheltered positions. A sentinel heron, his head down between hunched shoulders, kept watch stoically at the water's edge, beneath over-arching, feather-topped reeds. Once he stretched his neck and opened his beak in a sort of yawn then subsided into immobility again, an object lesson in patience. For a long time he stared into the water as if hoping to fathom the meaning of life. He ignored a moorhen sculling by, then a colourful shoveler drake, then a small party of coots, which came out of the water on to the narrow grass margin to peck for morsels like black-coated philosophers going over old ground in the hope of some new discovery. The heron ignored them all, keeping up his solitary vigil, fixed and statue-like, his only movement the flicking of his head plumes by the restless wind.

Then, at last, there was a sudden flurry of movement as the long and powerful neck shot out and the dagger bill stabbed the water, pulling out a large and energetically protesting eel. In its struggles to break free the eel coiled itself round the head, beak and neck of the heron, until writhing eel and sinuous bird neck were one knotted, twisting mass of powerful muscle containing, inevitably, the force which was to conquer and the force which was to be extinguished. An experienced fisherman, the heron played the eel by holding on firmly and letting it tire itself by its struggles to escape.

At length he thought it safe to drop the eel to the ground, where, before it could wriggle away, he could give it several more stabs until it was quiet enough to be swallowed. Inch by inch the snake-like fish disappeared into the heron's capacious gullet, and when the tail end had finally vanished and the eel was already suffocating in the dissolving juices of his stomach, the big bird gulped, stared, swallowed hard again and became a statue once more. Though not for long.

After a while he walked solemnly about on the narrow strip of reed margin to aid the digestion of his big catch. He wiped the eel's slime off his beak on a reed stem, dipped his beak into the water and drank, then spread his broad wings and with a satisfied 'kronk' sailed off into the implacable winter wind.

12 December

The wind had dropped considerably this morning, and there were tracts of thick cloud in the sky, but there were also patches of blue and the air was still cold, with tiny pockets of frost on the lawns. I wrapped up well and went out to stack a load of cherry logs that a kind friend had given me. It was warm work on a cold day, stacking next to the dry, grey logs left from the felling in January this freshly cut cherry wood, with its purplish, freckled bark and red-ringed heartwood like the auras of remote, austere and wonderful planets. As I worked I became aware of being watched, and looked up to see Cedric eyeing me from the cover of a hazel thicket not far away. He gave a series of crowing calls, so when I had finished with the log pile I scattered some seeds and watched him in turn as he came down for his breakfast. Later his new hen turned up, the pale one which we have seen in the garden all autumn. She looks like being his first choice for the start of next season, a replacement for the late, lamented Hetty and Hatty, both no longer with us, alas. We shall call her Hazel. The relationship for now is an uncertain one, because of the time of year. Cedric grudgingly allows her to feed but circles her closely all the time, dropping his wing and puffing up his feathers, giving a display which looks to be part courtship, part warning.

13 December

Dark until after eight o'clock, the sun coming over the ridge at about a quarter to nine, a fiery orange ball sending long, probing fingers of light through the wood. A great spotted woodpecker came to the bird table at first light. He landed as usual with a faint clatter of strong claws on the upright post of the table, the preferred method of landing. I say 'he' because although, as with a range of species from robins to shelducks, it is hard to tell the sexes apart, the distinctive bright red patch on the nape of the neck is a feature only of the male. Otherwise they look the same, at least to me. They are very boldly marked birds, and at close quarters it is easy to see just how splendid they are, both sexes wearing a harlequin costume which is all white on the front, black on the back and wings with conspicuous spots, bars and patches, and petticoat red underneath the tail.

This individual quickly climbed up the table's supporting pine post, tapping half hopefully for grubs lurking beneath the flaking bark and, finding none, moving rapidly onto the table top, where he stood squarely in the middle rapping the hard wood and sounding it out. There was nothing doing, so he began to feed on soft oats and hard grain. When other birds attempted to land he drove them away with spread wings and a sharp beak. The wings are spread out both as a threat and to make it harder for a new arrival to land. In this way the persistent chaffinches were seen off, also the one-legged starling, which sought solace on the smaller, covered bird-table close against the kitchen wall. Even a jay sheered off when he tried to land, and he is a much bigger bird, so it would seem that size is less important in the defence of one's feeding place than the bird's presence on it. Possession is nine tenths of the law.

Blackbirds are now more numerous at the feeding tables than they were, probably an influx of migrants. All the birds have to be quick off the mark to be able to eat enough to sustain themselves through eighteen hours of darkness, three-quarters of the daily cycle. At half past three the sun is going down again, an even bigger orb of fire cutting a crimson path across the sea and turning the grey face of Trowbarrow cliff a blushing pink. While there is light even the bank voles grow bolder, rushing out from their snug nests under the ferns and running about inches from our window, then whisking back again with a bit of wheat or sunflower seed. They are supposed to be torpid in the cold weather, but perhaps this vole has not read the text books. This activity on the part of small rodents is good news for owls, kestrels, buzzards and the like, who feed so largely on them. Also the increasing number of molehills in the fields (and on the lawns) is a good sign from their point of view. People seldom see a mole, but the buzzards catch them all the time, and there are recorded instances of them forming the bulk of their diet.

16 December

On any of the sunnier, warmer days there are always a few insects to be seen, such as the swarms of gnats which were very active along the banks of Hawes Water today. There were bees, too, busy collecting pollen among the masses of small yellow flowers now out all over the ivy clumps. It is a fine sight, somehow reassuring, to see bees buzzing in an ivy bunch on a sunny day in winter. It is often said that the ivy is the last plant to flower in the year and the first to fruit and it is vital to those bees awoken by the temporary warmth. Among the flowers there are green, unripe ivy berries formed, and a few black ones already ripe. They provide a welcome breakfast for the woodpigeons, which love them and scramble all over the tops of ivy clad walls, as well as in the tree tops, great blue-grey birds clumsily flapping among the topmost twigs where the berries are.

17 December

They are burning reeds at Leighton Moss. Long, scarcely moving curtains of white smoke drift down the valley so slowly that the mistake at first is that it is a sea fog or mist off the marshes. It isn't, and the smell of burning soon gives the game away: another stage in the yearly cycle of maintaining the Moss as a richly diverse habitat, one of the foremost wetlands in the country, where scarce and intriguing specimens of plant and animal life are nurtured and encouraged.

Previous generations harvested the reed for thatching and other purposes, but the development of the roads and railways brought a ready supply of ready-cut slates and machine-made tiles of uniform size for every local roof, and thatched roofs fell out of use almost everywhere, associated as they were with humble peasant dwellings. The small amount of reed cut on the Moss every year thus has little or no commercial value, and so is burned on the spot.

The reed burning is a job for the professionals, who know exactly what they are doing and control the fires with great care. As I watched their activities with interest I reflected on the willingness of volunteers over the years and importance of their freely-given labour in the maintenance and development of Leighton Moss. I remembered again my first visits to Silverdale, thirty years ago, as one of a party of volunteers. The Warden, John Wilson, used our labour gratefully and effectively, always encouraging and guiding us, never impatient at any clumsiness or inexperience on our part. Plenty of work got done. I spent very little time on the Moss watching birds in those days, being mostly involved in helping in a small way to make the Reserve what it is today. As well as the path laying I remember standing in muddy water, clearing the ditches that cut through the soft, dark moist peat.

I helped in clearing some of the willow scrub, too. 'Why does conservation work always involve cutting down trees?' a volunteer was heard to ask on one occasion. The answer was ready to hand. One of the advantages of being involved in such work is that you not only know you are doing good work, but why it is so important. A balance between reed and water has to be maintained, with a few trees and thickets of low-growing willows for shelter, nest sites, etc. If the willow encroaches too much, the ground dries out and will eventually become woodland. Similarly the reedbeds, left undisturbed, encroach on the open water, which is essential for all the birds on the Reserve, even the secretive, reed-loving bittern. Hence the smoke drifting down the valley.

18 December
A cold day with a severe frost. The sun hardly rose above the tree tops, so that even on our afternoon walk there were large tracts of frost unthawed. Sedges and grasses were bowed down with the frost, curved and whitened like the frost patterns on the ice puddles. Even the ditch beside the path at Silverdale Moss was covered with ice where it ran, or rather stood, under a protecting canopy of bushes. A snipe was searching for a patch of unfrozen mud to probe with its long beak, but started up away from us in its zigzag flight when we came too near. Seven blackbirds came to our bird table, also a flock of goldfinches, and a reed bunting has returned to us much earlier than usual. At night in the wood the light of a bright moon was reflected on the frost-blanched branches.

20 December
Dawn breaks later and later for another day or two, but the eastern sky is brilliant with scarlet then gold, to compensate us for the tardiness of the day, the bitter cold, and the grey gloom which spreads when the sun has risen into the clouds.

22 December
Following a thaw the fields at Crag Foot are flooded, and thickly populated by wading birds, mostly flocks of knot and dunlin with some oystercatchers and curlew, all paddling about like bank-holiday crowds, busy in their own world just feet away from the road and its traffic. The small waders take off in huge flocks and circle the valley like smoke in the wind as an enormous sun looms out of the mist.

Christmas Eve
The shortest day of the year has come and gone, so we can look forward to lengthening days from now on, but there is no perceptible improvement yet, and the day was thoroughly overcast. Laggard daylight only comes at a quarter to nine, but there are signs and portents to be seen, a few weeds in flower such as groundsel, and a couple of daisies on the lawn. I like the old saying about it being spring when you can cover five daisies with your foot. That is a long way off, but, for now, two is good.

Christmas Day
A family of long-tailed tits appeared, a dozen of them all at once among the bushes at the front of the house, swinging on the ball of fat, pecking at peanuts and sunflower hearts. They were probably a complete family, survived this far into the winter at least. They are such fragile-looking little birds, as if a puff of icy wind would blow them to pieces, and certainly they are very vulnerable in cold weather, like all small birds. Probably no more than half of this company will survive until the spring, but for now they move about

the village and the woods as one, having started life together in a tiny nest no bigger than a large orange, a ball of feathers, moss and grasses where no nestling so much as moved a muscle without affecting its fellows. Of all days in the year, this is one where the closeness of families is thought of and encouraged, and here was a reminder of the universal principle of family unity.

26 December

After the orgy of shopping has run its course, like some communal sacrifice to an implacable god of getting and spending, the real Christmas season brings the cure for the excess of materialism. The human frame needs its time of repose just as the human spirit needs time for prayer and reflection, and this occurs at just the same time that nature is at its quietest, conserving its strength, preparing itself for a new cycle of growth and reproduction. So it was that a profound stillness wrapped the land like a blanket this morning, a remarkable tranquility even for this normally quiet bit of countryside. When the distant gunfire of a Boxing Day shoot started up later in the morning, it did little to dispel the mood, except for those unfortunate pheasants, expensively reared as ready-made moving targets, which fell prey to the guns. It was noticeable how closely our own pheasants kept to their home ground this afternoon, feeding close to the house then making a stately progress up into the wood in search of somewhere to roost as daylight began to fail. Feeding pheasants, eager sportsmen and holiday walkers alike all ceased their activities by four o'clock, by which time the fire was lit and we were enjoying the heat and the flickering flames of crackling logs of birch, ash and cherry.

29 December

A pair of collared doves come into the garden nearly every day to feed, always in the afternoon by which time the other birds have been at the tables for four or five hours of the short span of daylight. There is still a little left for them, and they eat their fill of course, but already their minds are on other things, and while all other species are turning their attention to the warmth and relative security of their nightly roost, the female dove runs along the ground with short steps as her crooning, pouting mate pursues her. Their breeding season is a long one, lasting from March to September, but individual pairs may start breeding as early as February if the weather is mild, and this pair clearly seemed of the opinion that a little courtship practice would not come amiss. It is this precociousness that has led to the pigeon tribe being as prolific and successful as it has. The half-tame, half-wild pigeons of our towns and cities, descended from the wild rock dove and usually referred to as the feral pigeon, are the supreme example of this tendency. I have seen their eggshells on the ground at the front of St. John's Church on New Year's Day indicating newly hatched pigeon squabs in the tower above. It just isn't possible to begin the breeding season any earlier than this.

New Year's Eve

A heavy frost again overnight and bitterly cold this morning. At a quarter to nine the sun was touching trees on the hill in the distance at Slackhead, then soon afterwards the treetops in Eaves Wood. No snow on the high ground of Arnside Knott, Warton Crag, Farleton Knott and Clougha, and only a dusting of it, like flour on a loaf of bread, on the Lakeland hills visible across the Bay. The bare trees raise their branches to heaven, gripping the limestone that is the backbone or the skeletal frame of this special land. Stripped of vegetation the trees and bushes, the rocky ground itself, all stand revealed in their essential unity of purpose, the flowing together and the branching out of the energy of the universe. There is, it has long been said, a correspondence of patterns and shapes in nature, not merely a coincidence but a sign or index of all creation which is there for those to read it who will, whether for scientific or spiritual reasons. The veins in a leaf and in an old man's hand, a river's tributaries and its estuary, ranges of hills joining and parting; these things are both a symbol of the oneness of nature and part of its diversity. Some modern theoreticians and mathematicians believe this apparently random correspondence of forms to be the true geometry, deeper than the familiar Euclidean one based on squares, circles, cubes and cones.

In the wood I stood among the rusty, brown and shrivelled leaves, and picked up one to examine it. It was an oak leaf. As it lay, tan coloured and papery in the palm of my hand, I thought how like a hand it was itself, its lobed edges like stubby fingers, its narrow paths and channels, now empty of life, so like human veins. I remembered that John Ruskin, the Sage of Coniston, saw a leaf not as an emblem of the brevity of life, but as a symbol of the constant renewal of things, and all around us that process of renewal is going on, mostly hidden from our eyes but, for all that, the most potent of natural forces. In the red berries of the holly bush there is not just a reminder of the good fellowship of the season, there is the promise of more holly trees in the wood in years to come.

'Nature knows no calendar,' wrote Flora Thompson, the author of '*Lark Rise to Candleford*', that remarkable autobiography and study of Victorian village life. She pointed out that even as the leaves fall all around us, next year's buds are formed. They wait in readiness for the quickening of life, for the warmth of the sun's rays to strengthen and the sap to rise. Already on the hazel bushes there are short, hard, rigid protuberances, grey-green with a pinkish tinge, which when the time is right will become next spring's dangling, breeze-dancing yellow catkins. Even the unpromising, hard, black, sharp-pointed buds of ash, which look sculpted out of jet rather than a product of natural growth, are poised, stored with the sun's unfailing energy, ready to make their appearance on the scene.

As the rays of the setting sun filtered feebly through the trees, the last of the dying year, there was only the possibility of looking ahead, of getting on with the business of living. The pheasant, Cedric, crowed his approval of the sentiments as he went to roost. The brown owl seemed to agree as well, appearing suddenly in the wood on noiseless wings, to make his steady, silent, purposeful evening circuit. Suddenly I saw a roebuck, too, which had ceased grazing and had probably been watching me for some time with that steady stare of appraisal. It was if he represented the whole of nature at that moment, intent on survival, watchful and wary of man and his dangerous and unpredictable ways. We looked at one another for some time. One of us would have to make a move, and rather than disturb the deer, which belonged in the wood more than I did, I turned and then went indoors.

Jenny Brown's Point

If you have enjoyed this book you may also enjoy other books published by Helm Press.

'A Westmorland Shepherd' His life, poems and songs

'Elephants On The Line' Tales of a Cumbrian Railwayman

'Dear Mr Salvin' The story of the building of a 19th century Ulverston church

'All In A Lifetime' The story of a Dalesman as told to June Fisher

'Hawkshead Revisited A Walk in time through Hawkshead

'A Century of Heversham and Leasgill' A walk in time through these old Westmorland villages

'An Old Westmorland Garage' The story behind Crabtree's of Kendal

'Ambleside Remembered' People and Places, Past and Present

'Snagging Turnips and Scaling Muck' The Women's Land Army in Westmorland

'The Windermere Ferry' History, Boats, Ferrymen & Passengers

'Kendal Green' A Georgian Wasteland Transformed

'Kendal Brown' The History of Kendal's Tobacco & Snuff Industry

'On & Off the Rails' The Life of a Westmorland Railwayman

'Stainton. An Old Westmorland Parish' Reminiscences of a local farmer

'Jack's Lad' The life of a Westmorland Agricultural Contractor

10 Abbey Gardens, Natland, Kendal, Cumbria LA9 7SP
Tel: 015395 61321
E-mail: HelmPress@natland.freeserve.co.uk
www.natland.freeserve.co.uk